The Best of

Ms. Gaines,

Anybody who loves essays as much as you do is Bubba to the core.

Pat Joh

Happy Birthday!

Kim & Meg

Gary & Pat

HUB CITY

19 98

The Best of Radio Free BUBBA

ISBN 1-891885-03-0
First printing, November 1998

Hub City editors, John Lane and Betsy Wakefield Teter
Cover/book design and photography Mark Olencki
Cover radio image suggested by Terry Ferguson. Cover radio is
  a Truetone Super Heterodyne equipped with Truetone
  Stratoscope. Cover radio owner is Greg Olle, owner of Java Jive
  Coffeehouse and Cafe in downtown Spartanburg, South Carolina.
  Cover radio environment provided by Java Jive, too.

Hub City Writers Project
Post Office Box 8421
Spartanburg, South Carolina 29305
(864) 577-9349 • fax (864) 577-0188 • www.hubcity.org

PLAYLIST

FOREWORD . . . FORWARD!

"Hey! Are you a Bubba?" I am yelling this out of the car window while stopped at the World's Longest Traffic Light in Rutherfordton, North Carolina. I am yelling it at the curly-headed man in the pickup truck inches ahead. The summer heat of 1990 has put the world behind an antique windowpane. Everything is wavering, like some kind of weird, mechanical ocean. The bumper stickers on the tailgate ahead are puckering, but legible. One reads: "It's Not Up To Somebody Else." It is the reason I am yelling out of my car window at a strange man.

I know the slogan well, as its twin had appeared on my desk at WNCW not long after I began work there as news director in May 1990. It was left by one Pat Jobe, a.k.a. "Bubba." My instincts tell me the man ahead is one and the same, or related through Bubba-ism or by blood. At this point in time, I have never met Bubba Pat in the flesh, but I already know we are both listening to the same radio station!

The curly head pokes out of the truck window, and I hear, "Yeah!" There is a slight pause. The light does not change. Then a slightly astonished profile twists around, and he hollers, "Are you a Bubba, too?" He motions me towards a nearby parking lot. We pull over, and we hug.

My husband, Randy, was introduced to Bubba Pat

while both men were training for one of those jobs you take to tide you over. That brief term of employment brought us a new refrigerator and a flurry of issues of *The Bubba Newsletter*. We still have both, one in the kitchen and the other in the file cabinet. The newsletters were modest, two-page missives, published on recycled paper by a handful of Bubbas for a slightly larger group of ad-hoc and would-be Bubbas. The circulation grew one reader at a time, and subscriptions could be had for the price of postage and printing. Newsletter content ranged from items headlined "Governor Holds Fate of Battered Wife" to "Paper Bag Poetry." In 1989 and early 1990, *The Bubba Newsletter* was the only thing waiting for us in our mailbox besides bad news.

We made it through those hellish years of births, deaths, and lupine bill collectors comforted by kindred spirits—Bubbas—nearby. It was like we all had taken an unwilling vow of poverty and, together, were slowly being distilled into better human beings by life's daily disasters. The newsletter could make you feel all right about that. It gave us reminders of the women in shelters, foster kids, and the fact that there were Bubbas out there trying to make a difference. It reminded me that my Grandmother says, "There is always somebody worse off than you."

The term "Bubba" surely originated here in the South among very young children who could not verbalize all the consonants in the word "Brother."

The use of the word "Bubba" in our chosen context extends the family. It affectionately denotes the kinship we feel towards folks who are unafraid to reach out a helping hand to a stranger in need or to speak out for what is right.

Radio Free Bubba, which is carried on WNCW (88.7 FM) public radio in Spindale, North Carolina, was a sequel to the newsletter, but one that was better than its predecessor. It was better because it brought the message to more people and expanded the Bubba kingdom. Pat Jobe apparently recognized the potential vehicle, and the folks involved in the process of creating a radio station recognized a great title when they heard one. WNCW signed on the air on Friday, October 13, 1989, and soon, Radio Free Bubba and the provocative thoughts of Pat and Kim Taylor became a gentle hand that guided us all.

We were pioneers, and every radio day was a wagon train into the wilderness. News of our voyage spread one person at a time, and as we gained listeners, we also gained two new Bubba voices, Meg Barnhouse and Gary Phillips.

It was a trip made with a lot of care and planning. We dared not disrupt the emotional ecosystems, nor encroach upon the habitats of the heart without love. Our mission at WNCW was simple: to bring alternative news, thought-provoking commentary, and little-heard music to the heretofore-deprived nooks and crannies of western North Carolina. Getting into several other states was an unforeseen bonus. I don't think any of us ever spoke a word or played a tune without considering who might be on the receiving end of it all.

Every Wednesday morning for six years at about 8:45 a.m., I had the pleasure of introducing Radio Free Bubba. I rarely failed to sit in the control room and listen myself. I think now I needed to be reminded that I belong to a tribe. To be a Bubba, you don't have to carry a card, survive a hazing, or pass a test. Pat, Kim, Meg, and Gary are Bubbas; therefore we are Bubbas, too. The only criteria are to be a member of the human race and not be perfect. And if there is a Bubba slogan, it is surely "It's Not Up To Somebody Else."

I have moved on, but the Bubbas have not; they still broadcast weekly from WNCW. My bumper sticker now resides at the head of our family bulletin board. It is foremost among the pictures, school reminders, and spider webs. I could never bring myself to stick it on anything permanently. Cars and guitar cases come and go. In case of fire, it's at the top of my list—along with children and photo albums— to grab on the way out of the door! It has long been the only tangible reminder that, yes, I am a Bubba.

Now we both have this book. I am joyful that this collection did not go the way of so many other moments released onto the radio airwaves. These words did not just bounce off our beautiful mountains and eventually out into the ozone and beyond. Our journey did not go unnoticed or unrecorded. *The Best of Radio Free Bubba* goes from our hearts to yours. Give one to a friend. Bubbahood is powerful!

—*Wanda Lu Greene, June 1998*

GETTING A GRIP

Meg Barnhouse

The morning was dull and cold. The color of the sky was the gray of a '74 hearse I saw priced to sell in a front yard last Tuesday up on the Chesnee Highway. I put on my raincoat by the front door, being careful to protect my right thumb as I slid my arm into the sleeve. The pain had brought me to my knees a couple of times when I accidentally knocked it against something. It was time to take the boys to school. We were running late because every little thing I had to do in the morning took five times as long without the use of my thumb. I brushed my hair left-handed, asked the kids to make their own breakfasts, and turned the key awkwardly in the car's ignition by holding it between my first and second fingers.

After dropping the boys at school, I headed downtown to the coffee shop looking for my minimum daily requirement of Blue Ridge Blend and companionship. It's not only the coffee to which I'm addicted. It's the people who are sitting in there. I walked in, and Jack, the owner, called out "Good morning, Meg!" Nearly everyone else said, "Hey, Meg." I see these same people most mornings. I can call most of them by name. There's Tim, who has the sixth volume of Sandburg's biography of Lincoln propped in front of him on the bar. Phil sits next to him, reading the paper. There is Stephen, who is rebuilding a Corvair in his garage, and Bill, who likes to give shoulder rubs and calls all women "beautiful." Trish, a massage therapist who actually *is* beautiful, sits at the bar, too.

I walk past them to the table we have named the Center of the Universe. It sits in the narrow part of the long room after you pass the coffee bar. My friends gather there. Postcards from all over are taped up on the wall by the table. When any of us goes away, we send something back to the Center of the Universe. These are the regulars at the Center of the Universe:

Mack is a smooth storyteller and famous marinader of meat. Gary is a writer I like to talk to about sex. We enjoy trying to shock each other. It is not mature. John is a poet; Betsy's a publisher. Dee teaches two-year-olds and brings us feta cheese from her sister's goat farm. Her husband, Clarence, is crazy about computers and makes fiber optic cable on the night shift. There are two other ministers besides me, one arts administrator fresh from the Northwest, and a Hungarian ex-model and radio personality. Most of us do some writing. That is what first united us. Now it is time and habit and love.

I was complaining to my friends about my thumb. I sprained it, stupidly, in karate class. It had been a week since then, and my thumb still wasn't working. It was affecting my grasp of things. I couldn't get a grip. It was driving me crazy.

It is good to sit at the table before work, joking and talking about sex, politics, and religion. Our Southern town provides plenty of fuel for all those conversations. My friends were giving me satisfying sympathy for the pain in my thumb, especially the one who thought I said I had a pain in my bum.

On my way out the door, I stopped to talk to Bill and Trish at the bar. They asked how I was, so of course I told them about my hurt thumb. Trish took my hand in hers. She offered to massage my arm so the blood would flow and make my thumb heal faster. I sat between the two of them, Trish working the muscles of my arm and Bill rubbing my neck. I felt loved. "We've got to take care of our Meg," he said. I could see the color coming to the surface of my skin as the muscles warmed up and let go. Trish started to work gently with my hand and then with my hurt thumb. I tightened up, expecting pain, then relaxed and trusted her. It was good. I was surrounded by friends. The coffee shop became sacred ground.

It is a holy thing to be heard, to be touched, to laugh and plot mischief and tell awful jokes, to show up morning after morning until you are known. It is a holy thing to sit with friends, stirring milk into coffee, giving stirring speeches, stirring things up until you are an ingredient in the recipe of one another's lives.

I was grinning as I walked out to my car. I could move my thumb. It was part of my life again. The day felt warmer and softer. The sky was really more the color of pewter than the color of a hearse. Or maybe it looked like a dove's wing. A dove's wing—that was more the color of things.

PIZZA DELIVERY

_____ Kim Taylor

Once, for a brief but extremely meaningful and impoverished period, I delivered pizzas. Delivering pizzas is one of those jobs that if you haven't done it, you can't really appreciate it.

My roommate, Annette, got me into this noble profession. Annette's mother works answering the phone for one of the best pizzerias you could hope to find anywhere. It is a family business. Need I say more?

Annette and I decided to take the team-approach to pizza delivery. Annette handled the pizzas and the money. I drove the get-away car.

We showed up a little early our first night to be trained. Our boss met us with our "bank," told us how much money was in there, and said, "Get there as fast as you can without getting killed and don't tilt the pizzas." She smiled.

"That's it. That's our training?" I asked.

She laughed, "Yeah, you don't tilt the pizzas because the cheese will slide off."

It was fairly obvious why she didn't want us to get killed—it's hard to find replacement drivers.

We sat down in a row of metal folding chairs and waited for red, insulated bags with directions and prices taped to the top. Drivers, as we were called, often spend as much time waiting as they do delivering pizzas. But waiting can prove to be very interesting.

We learned a lot from Annette's mom. Carolyn is a sweet and wonderful woman, and we make fun of her often. She seems to take it fairly well. Answering the phone, taking directions from people who obviously don't know where they live, giving those directions to drivers, making change, and waiting on people who come in to pick up pizzas was a tougher job than we had realized. Friday and Saturday nights, the phones would ring faster than they could make and deliver pizzas.

Carolyn always asked that the people waiting for their pizzas leave a porch light on. She had hoped that might make finding a house a little easier.

One night, Annette and I found a house because we saw a woman standing in a kitchen chair changing her outside light.

I found out some things about people in general that I'm not sure I wanted to know. First of all, most people don't know where they live. They don't know if they live on the right or left side of the road. I love directions that read, "Only new trailer on the road." At 10 p.m., it is usually very dark. I don't know if it's a character flaw, but I can't seem to tell the age of anything when I can't see it.

Blue-collar folks tip better than white-collar. And boys get tipped more than girls—regardless of their age. Annette and I had to deliver several pizzas to a factory. We had to get out of the car, get through security, have the guy paged, wait about 15 minutes for Mr. Necktie to tear himself away, and we did not get a tip. I felt New York Waitress Syndrome coming over me. I wanted to grab his necktie and ask him if he thought we "girls" were delivering pizzas because we were bored and couldn't get dates.

My favorite pizza story has to do with an order Carolyn once took. She got a call from a woman who had ordered a pizza with no onions. Somehow, Carolyn had gotten confused and written "extra onions" on the order. The woman was calling to point out the error and see if it could be rectified. Carolyn frowned slightly and said, "Can't you pick 'em off?"

As we drivers were falling out of our metal folding chairs with laughter, one of the owners was diving for the phone. The onion lady got a free pizza, and we got a story that carried us through several rainy, mud-dy nights of green trailers on the right side of the road after the third brown house with a barn and a blue Monte Carlo in the driveway.

COOKING WITH CATS

Pat Jobe

Let me risk hurting my wife's feelings and the feelings of all you cat lovers out there. One of the things I like least about my present life is cooking with cats. Sleeping with cats is really not so bad except when they want to come in or out at 3 a.m., which does happen almost every morning. Reading or playing a game with cats is not so bad except when they want to take a nap between you and whatever you're trying to read or play.

But cooking with cats leaves me yearning for a third arm, an arm that would serve no other purpose than swatting, lifting, pitching, shooing, thumping, and shaking my fist at the cats.

I know how you cat lovers are. You hate me already, but in my defense, may I say that I have never thumped a cat. I have, however, swatted, lifted, pitched, shooed, and shaken my fist at cats.

We live with five cats. We had six, but Tigger couldn't take the stress. We suspect he committed suicide or blessed some catless household with his delightful nature. I kid you not, sports fans. He was the least obnoxious of the six. Number five on the least obnoxious list is Frosty, whom I expect to die any day. Cats are like people. The meaner they are, the longer they live. Number four is Jessica, a queen, usually silent and cooperative.

Among my three worst cats is Grandma Kitty. So named because not only has she given birth, but her issue have given birth. Yes, humane society zealots, all our females are now fixed, and only the male remains to have his attitude surgically adjusted.

Never has there been a male more deserving of castration. This boy has hidden a private stock of testosterone, and he mainlines the stuff when nobody's looking. His name is Alexander, and there's no need to add THE GREAT to his moniker. He knows he's great, and he'll whip you to prove it.

Finally, there is Grandma Kitty's daughter, Tobias. When we named her, we didn't know that her name means "God with us," but now we do. That's such a lovely sentiment. Unfortunately this cat has left the "with us," off her name and thinks it simply means "God."

These three awful cats will come into the kitchen on the rare occasions I cook and drive me completely insane. As soon I get one off the counter, another jumps up. Heaven help me if I walk away from anything I'm cooking. The term "fair game" was invented to describe the way my cats feel about anything I'm cooking.

I occasionally boil large pots of water hoping one of them will accidentally fall in. Just kidding.

I recommend cooking with cats to anyone whose life has become so peaceful as to approach boring. Are you really good at meditation and relaxation? Do stress management companies ask you to demonstrate your mysterious smile and deep breathing? Have you healed people simply by walking into a room? If you answered yes to any of these questions and would like to be more like the rest of us, come to my house and cook with my cats. You'll discover there's a Nazi lurking in your soul, too.

TRYING TO BE THERE

Meg Barnhouse

Annie Dillard writes: "About five years ago I saw a mockingbird make a straight vertical descent from the roof gutter of a four-story building. It was an act as careless and spontaneous as the curl of a stem or the kindling of a star.

"The mockingbird took a single step into the air

and dropped. His wings were still folded against his sides as though he were singing from a limb and not falling, accelerating thirty-two feet per second, through empty air. Just a breath before he would have been dashed to the ground, he unfurled his wings with exact, deliberate care, revealing the broad bars of white, spread his elegant, white-banded tail, and so floated onto the grass. I had just rounded a corner when his insouciant step caught my eye; there was no one else in sight. The fact of his free fall was like the old philosophical conundrum about the tree that falls in the forest. The answer must be, I think, that beauty and grace are performed whether or not we will or sense them. The least we can do is try to be there."

I know beauty and grace are all around me. Sometimes I know how to be there for it. Other times I get distracted by dips and crashes in my bank balance, by my child coughing, my body aging, or by someone being disappointed in me somewhere in the world.

Usually it is clear, though, that I can make a choice to stew about things or to be there for my life. One of the teachers in my life is an Aikido Master named Wendy Palmer. She tells me in her book, *The Intuitive Body*, that I get what I pay for when I pay attention. Whatever I pay attention to, that is what I get. If I pay attention to the things that are nuisances, my life feels like one, big nuisance. If I pay attention to beauty and joy, my life fills up with beauty and joy. I get what I pay for.

Last weekend at Spartanburg's Spring Fling, I was paying attention to 90-degree heat and shoving crowds, standing in line at the bumper-car ride with my two boys. One of them kept changing his mind about whether he wanted to ride. What he really wanted to do was toss rubber chickens into a pot, five tries for two dollars. My brain was a rubber chicken. I had just dragged the children all over the fair looking for the writers with whom I was supposed to sign books and the folks from my church with whom I was supposed to sell beer. I couldn't find either group, and the whole time I was looking for those people, both boys were pulling on me asking, "Can we ride the rides now?" I didn't even have the energy to have the "do you know the difference between 'can' and 'may'?" discussion because last time, the nine-year-old said, "Yeah, mom, May is a month, and can is a tin container." Sigh. So I said, "Let's go ride the rides." Here we were in line, and into my head came this thought: "I am in hell."

When I saw my older son dive into a car and start manhandling the wheel, waiting for the ride to start, I moved into the shade with his brother to watch. There my brain cooled off enough to remember to enjoy my life, to be there for the beauty and grace in that situation. I saw my son's mouth open wide with joy, its inside stained red by tiger's-blood-flavored shaved ice. He was in a state of bliss, being slammed from behind and from all sides by other bumper-car drivers. He threw back his head and laughed, putting the pedal to the metal in reverse, snapping his head forward as he took aim, and slammed into another car, looking sideways at the other driver, grinning, not quite able to believe this was actually allowed. Jubilee. Bubbles of joy changed my breathing. I was having fun. Here was beauty, and here was grace, and here I was in the middle of it. My heart became a mockingbird, and it sang.

CATS AND DOGS AND KIDS
———————————————————— Kim Taylor

As much as I weasel and whine about my dog, I really love him.

I went to the kitchen last night to do the dishes. Sometimes, I'm really good about "household chores," and then there are times when I wash the dishes only because I need a glass or a spoon or a bowl, and I might as well wash them all while I'm at it.

So I went into the kitchen where the dogs were corralled. They were enormously excited that I was in the kitchen. They skipped around my feet, wagging tails and grinning as best they could. I skipped around with them and grinned because I'm better at that than tail wagging.

Once I started washing dishes, they settled down in a corner somewhere nearby and just grooved on my proximity. I realized standing there, elbow deep in dishwater, why people have dogs. No person I know has *ever* been that happy to have me in the kitchen. And while I'd been very reluctant to go into the kitchen, after my happy puppy greeting, I was glad I made the trip.

Dogs are really great at that kind of unconditional hallelujah. I've heard people say that's why they prefer dogs to cats. I am not one of those people. I love my cats. I probably love your cats, too.

Someone once wrote that cats have already met all the people they care to know. A cat is interested in you for one of three reasons: 1) you are terrified of cats, 2) you have food, or 3) they really like you.

I have a cat who has been with me for 15 years. I've dragged that cat all over the state of North Carolina, forced her to endure some interesting lifestyles and living conditions, and still she stays. For the first 10 years, I thought she stayed just to torture me, but lately, I think she really likes me.

Jane—that's my cat—is purported to have a reputation across three states. If you look up "ornery" in the dictionary, her picture will be beside it. She is a white cat with one blue eye. She used to have two blue eyes, but she lost one in a fight with another white cat. My friend, Kit, said they fought because "they had on the same dress."

Jane thought we moved to the country for her retirement.

My cats and dogs are the living proof that I should not be a parent. They satisfy my maternal instincts, as meager as they are. And I don't have orthodontist bills or nightmares over drugs and Satanism.

Not having children is one of those things I've been sure of since before I was an adult. When I was younger, I found that stating I had no desire to have children was sometimes met with anger. Once, after arguing with me for half an hour over why I should have children, a woman screamed at me, "Who will take care of you when you are old?" (Twenty years ago, I heard a woman on TV say that we needed wars because they were good for the economy. I think these two women swam in the same gene pool.) I was so flabbergasted by her question, I'm not sure I answered it adequately.

As I stood washing dishes with cats and puppies round my feet, I remembered the red face and the anger of that day.

Hey Lady! Are you out there? I'll be 37 next month. And I still don't have babies, and I still don't want to. And in answer to your question—save me a seat in the nursing home.

WORD FROM ACROSS THE RIVER

Pat Jobe

When I first met Katie Ridgeway, I didn't know she was an angel. Now there's no doubt. Angels come from the land beyond the river. They bring word from on high, and they say life must be believed differently, status quo is headed out the window, a great storm is just around the bend, and we are not to take cover but dance in the wind. Miss Katie brings such word. It came on the night we were talking about some awful sin.

We talk quite a bit these days. She sits beside me in the front seat. Pre-teenagers ponder awful sins—especially the public ones like smoking, drinking (pronounced by many Southerners as dranking), and cussing. She had asked me about some combination of those and whether I do those things. When I told her no, she said, "I guess you're just one of those people who never does anything wrong."

"No," I corrected her. "I often do many things wrong. You just didn't happen to hit my list that time."

She sat for only a second thinking about that and then said, "Yes, that's right."

When I met her, she was about to turn five. Now she is 12, and for most of those seven years we have been an almost constant presence in each other's lives. Two years after we met, I married her mother, and the tenuous truce that exists between stepfathers and stepdaughters is ours until death us do part.

Her angelic word hit again as we talked of right and wrong. One of her sisters assaulted a neighborhood child with verbal brickbats. It sounded like above-normal levels of violence, so I gave a fatherly word.

"Please don't talk to other people that way, no matter what they may do to you. It's never okay to be mean and hateful," I said gently. From her angelic post near me, Katie said loudly enough for me alone to hear, "You sometimes do that."

Again. "Yes. That's right."

We talked another time about loyalty to ultimate truth, about living the best kind of life, and never being satisfied with anything less. I quoted an ancient sage who said everything he had accomplished in his life came to pee-turkey-squat compared to this good life, this true life, this race well run. Katie objected. She asked, "You mean my clarinet playing and my soccer playing don't count for anything?"

Not compared to total living, ultimate truth, love without conditions—at least according to the ancient one.

She said the ancient one might be wrong. I said maybe he had experienced some things she had not and told her I didn't judge her harshly for that. But I asked her to be open to more experiences, to seeing new things along her yellow brick road.

This is her great gift to me. With an impish grin and eyebrows that dance as well and wildly as the rest of her, she demands openness from me. Prepare yourself for more experiences. There are other sights to see, dragons to slay, demons to wrestle. Think not your life an auto-piloted jumbo-jet just because your belly is bigger and your nose is starting to grow. At 43, there is still new color in the sky, new cloud on the horizon, new hay in the field. You haven't seen it all. The best and maybe the worst is yet to come. But the best, the most impish grin, the dancingest eyebrows will win . . . in the end.

YADAMADIAN

_____ _Meg Barnhouse_

When friends come to visit me, I love showing them around this part of the South. It's beautiful, the people are fun, and there are lots of exotic sights and sounds.

My friend, Kathleen, was going through a time of transition in her life. She had been an opera singer, a shepherdess on an island in the Scottish Hebrides, a caterer, and a Presbyterian minister. She wanted to come for a visit, but she also wanted some time alone on a spiritual retreat. I had heard of a retreat center called Snail's Pace that was right outside of Saluda, North Carolina, so I picked her up from the airport, and we drove to Saluda.

There are people who like to have directions before they go somewhere new. They like to have a map in the car and reservations ahead of time. If you go off for a weekend with those people, they like to plan who will be responsible for which meals ahead of time. They pack as if there are no grocery stores where you're going, and they *hate* to hear things like "Don't worry, it'll all work out." They snarl, "I know it will work out. It will work out because I'll work it out!" These are people with a plan, and it is upon these people that civilization rests.

I am not one of those people. Sticking to a plan is torture for me. I am responsible when I need to be, which is most of the time, but sometimes I like to go on instinct and intuition. I persist in believing I have a sixth sense that helps me find places, even though it only works sporadically. It kicks in often enough to keep me hopeful, and it increases my odds of having a little adventure, which keeps me interesting to myself.

I didn't have directions to Snail's Pace, so we drove around Saluda following my sixth sense. It wasn't working at all. We finally stopped at a gas station to ask directions. I waited in the car, and Kathleen went in.

When she got back to the car, she was concentrating hard. She slid into the passenger seat and said, "I'm going to have to use my opera training here." Apparently, when singers memorize arias in languages they don't understand, they do it syllable by syllable. The North Carolina mountain accent had been as incomprehensible to her as Italian or German.

"I asked him for directions to Snail's Pace," she said, "and I did not understand a word he said. I'm going to repeat it back to you syllable by syllable. Maybe you'll understand it."

"Okay, let's try," I said. I am half-Southern by birth, and I have lived here for years. All the accents of the South are music to my ears.

"Gonuppaire," she began. "Tike rot."

"Uh, huh." I was with her so far. "Go on up there, take a right."

"Yadamadian."

"Yadamadian?" I repeated.

"That's what he said. It sounds like an Armenian name. Are there any Armenians up here?" she asked.

"Not that I know of."

"Yadamadian, tike layuff."

"Yadamadian—yr at a madian. Madian—median! I've got it! Take a left at the median!"

"Guppaire cautermah, sawn layuff, cain missit."

"Go up there a quarter mile, it's on the left, you

can't miss it!"

We found it with no other difficulties. I love having adventures in exotic places.

THUNDERING INTO CHARLOTTE

Pat Jobe

In 1994 our radio family grew to include folks in Charlotte, North Carolina, who once only heard a crackling hint of our true selves on 88.7. Then we began thundering into the Queen City on 100.7 FM, and boy, were we proud of it. I told George Shibiner, who produced Radio Free Bubba for a while, that I was going to do a piece on being heard in Charlotte.

"Git yore grammar rite, boy," he admonished me and added, "Them's big city folks in Charlotte."

Well, George, I worked in Charlotte for three months, and I can assure you the residents of Metrolina are no more sophisticated than us "public radiators" up here in Spindale.

Case in point. I was on an elevator in Charlotte with two energetic and folksy women who just carried on about how they were both from West Virginia.

They had met at a party with a whole slew of expatriate Mountain Staters and were enthralled to have reacquainted themselves on that there elevator. They just couldn't believe how many people who used to live in West Virginia now lived in Charlotte. Finally my mischievous nature got the best of me, and I said, "Yeah, I heard they're thinking about closing I-77."

A long, heavy silence settled over the occupants of the elevator, and for just a moment, I feared hospitalization might loom in my immediate future. Finally, one of them cut her eyes at me and said, "West Virginia's the best durn thing that ever happened to this town," and I laughed, and she laughed, and Providence allowed the elevator to reach my floor.

I also love to tell my small-town friends about the day I was standing in line in Charlotte with some local residents and struck up a conversation. You can tell this is a bad habit I have. I told them I was new to their city and praised their neighborhoods for having so many trees.

"Well, sir," said one of my companions, a tall, lanky, aging man. "It's the law around here. They don't let us cut down any trees."

I was amazed and almost lost my composure with praise for such a glorious law.

"To tell you the truth," he said, "I get tired of raking the leaves."

And to tell you the truth, we're mighty proud to be thundering into Charlotte, and we thank you for listening to our radio station. Put your radio out in the yard there, buddy, and you can tune us in while you rake those leaves.

THE FLU

_____ Kim Taylor

I'm just recovering from the flu, so that makes me the local expert. I'm just full of advice about the flu. Stuff like, how to know when you have the flu. The best clue I had was my earlobes hurt. I wasn't wearing clothespins on them. There was no reason for them to hurt. But they did.

Also, a little-mentioned but very obvious symptom of the flu is brain lock. All of a sudden, your old brain seizes up on you. Very sad. No aspirin—not even ibuprofen—will help that.

Most people wait until they start to experience flu symptoms before they go to the drugstore and try to find a cure. My advice is to go now, before you are sick. Once you get to the drugstore, you'll see why.

You'll cruise around to the cold remedies aisle, and there will be a crowd of people, mouths hanging open (because they can't breathe through their noses), staring mindlessly at the shelves. Their brains have locked. Some of them can't make a decision. Some of them can't remember why they are in the store. Just say, "Panty hose on aisle three" and give them a little nudge. They'll all just bunch off to aisle three. If it makes you feel guilty, once you've made your purchase, you can go to aisle three and announce, "Cold remedies on aisle five," and they'll all bunch back over there.

You'll get lots of advice about which cold remedies are best. As I've suggested, make these decisions before you become ill. And drop by the bank on your way to the drugstore.

I also advise trying to find someone to either stay with you while you have the flu or at least check in on you several times a day. Remember, you will be brain dead.

Don't go to the refrigerator alone. You'll open the door and get distracted by the lights and colors, and before you can remember why you're there, you'll get a chill.

I can't remember if you feed a cold or a fever. I say, eat what you can taste, which is another good reason to have someone looking out for you while you are sick. I ate what I could get to. But I don't want to talk about it.

Because I'm a world-class wimp, I strongly urge you to get those tissues with the lotion in them. Otherwise, after several days, your nose will glow, and you won't be able to touch it. And trust me, dabbing at it won't do the trick.

Loads of folks will tell you to see a doctor immediately. Hey, it's your life. Just remember, there are more sick people in the doctor's office than there are in the drugstore.

Stay away from nursing homes. There are signs on the door that say if you have flu symptoms not to come in. But your brain is vacationing somewhere warm and dry, and you'll go in anyway.

Oh, and avoid children. Not for their protection, but for yours. They're carriers. And I'm not convinced that they aren't in cahoots with the pharmaceutical companies.

There was some other stuff I wanted to tell you, but I can't seem to remember . . . What was I talking about?

MY INNER
MOTORCYCLE GANG

Meg Barnhouse

I get surly when someone tells me I've lost weight. It wakes up the rebel in me. I don't know why— maybe I don't like being on public display. Maybe it reminds me of the one time I went on a supervised diet. One time was enough; my good nature was almost ruined. It wasn't the salad and chicken breasts I lived on for two months, it was the diet supervisor and the idea of "being good."

For the three of you out there who have never dieted, "being good" means eating the things you are allowed and not eating the things you aren't allowed. The diet supervisor would weigh me three times a week in her office, tell me how much I had lost (or not), give me the little herb pills that were supposed to help me eat right, and take my money. If I hadn't lost, she'd ask, "Were ya bad?"

"No, I was good," I would answer through clenched teeth. "I just didn't eat the food I was supposed to." I know she got tired of hearing about my inherent goodness, but she kept asking the question. Maybe she decided never again to deal with dieting theologians or therapists, since they can't answer a simple question like "Were ya bad?" with a yes or no answer.

Once I asked her about the counseling that was advertised by the program. Their brochure said you could get counseling, and I needed some—I needed a lot, since I had been eating salad and chicken breasts for a month. "What do you mean, where's the counseling?" She was grieved. "I tell you how much you've lost, and I ask you how you're doing. That there's the counseling."

After weighing and paying, when I was headed out the door, she would call out to me, "Be good!" How can you respond to that? It made me feel like riding with the Hells Angels. It made me feel like piercing my nose and getting a tattoo of a large Neolithic goddess. Instead, I would snarl, "I *am* good," through clenched teeth, then I would get in my car and peel out of the parking lot.

I know some people don't have such a powerful a rebel streak that when someone says "be good," they have to moon the courthouse. I do. A couple of years ago, there was an ad before a movie in which a young actress sat in a bare room, spot-lit, and told the camera that crack cocaine was so deadly, compelling, and addictive that no one could try it without getting hooked. Once hooked, you would die. My best friend and I looked at each other in the dark and agreed that, even though it had never occurred to us up 'til now to do crack cocaine, after seeing that ad we felt an urge to take it up. The ad only ran briefly. Maybe they heard that crack sales were way up among movie-goers. I have a need to tell you that we never did try it, but for a moment I felt its appeal.

I know some of you have the rebel inside. When someone tells you the rules, you immediately want to break some of them.

I was in training with a Jungian analyst in Mill Spring when I had a dream about a motorcycle gang riding through my house, breaking things and ripping the rugs. My wise analyst looked at me with bright eyes and said, "Meg, you have to give those boys something to do." She told me the Harley riders were rebel elements in my psyche, and they were going to tear up my life if I didn't give them a job.

I assigned them the job of patrolling my life's boundaries. If someone tries to make me responsible for something that's not my responsibility, or if I'm being asked to do more than I can do, or if someone intrudes on me emotionally or spiritually, I hear the boys and girls in the biker gang start circling. V-r-r-r-o-o-o-o-m-m-m-m, v-r-r-r-o- o-o-m-m-m. They help me say "no," they help me keep safe, they help me let go of being compulsively sweet, and they laugh at the voices in my head that say I have to be thin to be good.

OATMEAL

_____ Kim Taylor

"But you haven't tried MY oatmeal."

A friend and I were taking care of a six-month-old. My friend carefully mixed some oatmeal and put a big spoonful in Baby's mouth. Baby immediately ejected it.

"Maybe it needs a little sugar," my friend said. I grinned and added a little sugar. Baby sucked off the sugar and ejected the oatmeal.

"My sentiments exactly," I stated.

"Don't you like oatmeal?" my friend asked.

No, I told her, I don't like oatmeal. And that doesn't mean I'm from another planet. I have a valid driver's license. I have no criminal record. I just don't like oatmeal.

It is scripted somewhere in that great library in the sky that if I say I don't like oatmeal, someone in the vicinity will say, "You haven't tried MY oatmeal."

Get a pencil. Here are some responses you might want to consider using:

"You haven't tried MY oatmeal."

I haven't driven your car, slept with your wife, or kicked your dog either.

"You haven't tried MY oatmeal."

No, and unless you have a recipe that turns oatmeal into ice cream, I'm not going to.

"You haven't tried MY oatmeal."

I'm holding out for the sushi-flavored instant.

Yes, Wilford Brimley seems like a nice enough fellow, and he likes oatmeal. Even if he does say it's the right thing to do—I'm not doing it.

Strangely enough, this oatmeal thing reminds me of water skiing. Every time anyone asks if I water ski, I say no. Because I don't. And then someone says,

"Well, that's because I'm not driving the boat."
(Actually, they say that just after they say, "You don't water ski?" ever so incredulously.)

People in the Piedmont say, "You don't snow ski?" in much the same way, but they preface it by saying, "You live in the mountains, and you don't snow ski?" Like it's a regional requirement. My new response to that will be, "You live in the Piedmont, and you don't grow tobacco?"

Anyway, several years ago, I was at a party out at Lake James. There were several boat owners there who kept trying to pressure people into water skiing. I made the mistake of saying, "I don't ski," instead of "No thank you." They would have been able to accept "no thank you" with no trouble. But the words, "I don't ski" brought something alive in them. Mainly, the desire to get me on water-skis.

By the end of the day, I couldn't take the pressure any longer. I think I screamed that I would try it just once, and then they better all leave me alone. I don't know how they decided who would be master of my fate, but I was soon encased in life-saving equipment (a reassuring gesture) and had skis strapped to my feet.

After being dragged all over Lake James, I let go. As they were dragging me into the boat, they were yelling, "Why didn't you stand up?"

Picture this: I've just had gallons of water in my face, in my eyes, and up my nose—not to mention getting about a 500-gallon enema. I'm bruised from being dragged into the boat, and some man is asking me why I didn't stand up.

What I wouldn't have given for some nice, hot oatmeal.

A WAITRE// IN THE /ACRED KITCHEN/

———————————————————— Meg Barnhouse

I love for a waitress to call me "Hon." It is comforting. She doesn't know me, and I don't know her, but we fit into well-worn, ancient categories: I am the Hungry One, and she is the One Who Brings Nourishment From the Unseen Source.

When I was younger, I worked as a waitress in Philadelphia and New Jersey. I learned things that have come in handy many times since then. I know how to rush around with my hands full, thinking about six things at once. That has stood me in good stead as the working mother of two small sons. I also realized that people are not at their best when they're hungry. That helps me understand world events; I know that if the citizens of the world were well fed, we'd have fewer wars and less mayhem.

The most useful thing I grasped while waitressing was that some tables are my responsibility, and some are not. A waitress gets overwhelmed if she has too many tables, and no one gets good service. In my life there are a certain number of things I have to take care of: I have my children, my relationships, my work, myself, and that's about it. Other things are not my table. I would go nuts if I tried to take care of everyone, if I tried to make everybody do right. If I went through my life without ever learning to say, "Sorry, that's not my table, Hon," I would burn out and be no good to anybody. It is necessary to my well-being to have a surly New Jersey waitress inside that I can call on when it seems everyone in the world is waving an empty coffee cup in my direction. My Inner Waitress looks over at them, keeping her six plates balanced and her feet moving, and says, "Sorry, Hon, not my table."

One of the hardest things for me to learn at the restaurant was how to blend into the woodwork. A man asked me once, "How long have you been here?" I smiled and said, "About five weeks, since the beginning of the semester . . ."

"I meant the *restaurant*," he interrupted. How humiliating. I grew up with parents who thought I was fascinating and smart, and they paid a lot of attention to me. I naturally assumed that someone could just look at me and want to know things about me.

What they needed was for me to fill a role, to be a function rather than an individual. I'm still learning this as a minister and as a therapist. It takes a certain spiritual strength for me to take on a role peacefully and let people relate to me in my function as a therapist or a minister, rather than as a fascinating woman with a birthday, a favorite color, a song I can sing better than it is performed on the album, and cool stories of travels to foreign lands. There is a loss of ego that's necessary before I can become willing to lose myself that way. I'm still not too good at it.

When I was in seminary learning to be a minister, all of us were struggling with how to blend and balance our individuality within the role of minister. We all found that most people have a strong idea of how a minister should look and talk and behave. I can be with a group of new people, talking and laughing, being normal, and the moment they find out I'm a minister, the laughter dies as they check back over the things they've said in front of me, trying to remember if they've sworn or sinned. It's hard. It makes some of us want to lie about what we do. It makes some ministers want to say the F-word just to eliminate those burdensome expectations.

There are times, though, when people need to draw strength and comfort from the Spirit, and I'm the one who is there at the hospital or at the funeral home in the role of minister. It is my job to bring nourishment to their hungry souls from the sacred kitchens where Spirit cooks up healing and comfort. It doesn't really matter at that moment when my birthday is, or that purple is my favorite color. What matters is the function I perform when I stand in the broad stream of history and symbol, faith and mythology, and let something larger than myself work its work through me. What matters is that I'm smelling the rich aromas of hope and joy rising from the dishes I hold in my arms, and that I know what it means to the people who are in need of that food I'm bringing for their souls. I like to remember where I began learning how to bring it to the table from the kitchen. Come sit down, Hon. Are you hungry?

ELVIS AND HUNGRY CHILDREN

Pat Jobe

What is the deal with this world-hunger trip? Just how many pictures of skinny kids with bloated bellies do we have to look at? Hand me the remote. Let's click to something else.

Along comes my beloved pal, the Rev. Mary John Dye, a brilliant writer and defender of all that's good in the universe. She tells me something I'd never heard before. Elvis was a hungry kid, even ate dirt as a little guy. She said one of his high-school teachers bought his lunch for over a year because the skinny guy was so obviously hungry.

Yowzer. *That* caught my attention. Elvis was *somebody*, the "Kang" for goodness sake, not some nameless, bloated belly with an oversized head and a flypaper mouth. Then my pal, Mary John, stretches me even further by saying we ought to use occasions like January 8, the Kang's birthday, and August 16, the day Elvis died, as dates to draw world attention to hungry children.

Oh, Mary John, I'm all shook up!

It gets worse, folks. Trust me on this.

My wife figures out that the cost of a small order of fries, about 80 cents, will save the life of 10 small fries in those bloated-belly pictures. UNICEF has come up with Oral Rehydration Therapy that will save a kid's life for eight cents.

So now, my sweetheart, Pam Jobe of Boiling Springs, South Carolina, is figuring everything in terms of hungry children. The cost of a movie ticket saves 75 kids. Instead of a cold beer, save 25 kids. What the average family spends at a Carolina Panthers game would save 2,500 babies. The cost of one skybox would fill their stadium with children saved from dehydration.

All of a sudden I can't breathe so well. Hand me

the remote. Click on something else.

Then I read that the net personal worth of all the people in the United States is $22 trillion. That, friends and neighbors, is a lot of money, more than they ever gave away in the Publisher's Clearinghouse Sweepstakes.

UNICEF says it can eliminate world hunger for $40 billion. That's what the world spends on golf. Holy catfish! So I get out my figuring pencil and break it down. If all us Americans are worth $22 trillion, and UNICEF only needs $40 billion, how much do each of us have to pitch in to get those babies off our TV screens and make Mary John and Pam talk about something else? This is amazing, folks. It really is. The percentage is 0.18. Not 18 cents out of your dollar, not 18 cents out of your $10 dollars, but 18 cents out of your $100.

Well, if that don't beat all! You mean, if we just all got together and mailed UNICEF $1.80 every time a thousand bucks passes through our bank accounts, we could eliminate world hunger?

I've got it!

How about a TV commercial where one of those bloated bellies looks right in the camera and sings, "Love me tender. Love me true. Never let me go-oh."

Nah!

Hand me the remote. Click on something else.

ALTERNATIVE TO GREED

Gary Phillips

Reading Rumi, the 13th-century Persian mystic poet, has become almost a daily tonic for me. I prefer the translation of Coleman Barks, who is Southern enough not to be afraid of religious language, and who has a deep sense of humor.

Rumi often writes about Nashrudin, a sort of half-comic, half-saint coyote, a trickster-figure of Muslim literature. One day, Nashrudin was eating his daily meal of chickpeas and bread when his puffed-up, next-door neighbor came by to harangue him.

"Nashrudin," he said, "you are such a tramp. Why don't you buy some new clothes and adopt finer manners? Look at me: I have a fine home, and I walk in important circles. If you learned to be subservient to the emperor like me, you wouldn't have to eat chickpeas and bread."

Nashrudin smiles. "If you learned to eat chickpeas and bread, you wouldn't have to be subservient to the emperor."

I think there is deep confusion in American life between the fruits of the inner life and the outer life. Our culture pretends there is no inner life, or worse yet, that it's a marketable commodity. If only we had the right things, we could be fulfilled, is the continual message of television and talk.

Last week, my local Ruritan Club met to honor the recipients of our annual scholarship grants. The teenagers were asked politely what they intended to do with their lives. One girl surprised us with, "I don't care as long as it makes lots of money."

Greed is pervasive in our culture. We are told now that shopping and TV are the favorite leisure activities of Americans, two sides of the same dangerous coin.

Greed is spiritually carcinogenic. Greed is incompatible with compassion.

We are wasting the earth's riches, making our cities uninhabitable, bombarding our children with advertising, furiously consuming and consuming and consuming our grandchildren's and our great grandchildren's inheritance. Our public actions do not match our inner feelings; they have an architecture of despair and self-destruction.

We covet what we see advertised. We invest in what promises the greatest return. Sweepstakes and lotteries and other promises come to us in the mail every day. To participate in public culture is to breathe this in and out.

And yet we are filled with a deep spiritual hunger. Is there an alternative to a life filled with greed and acquisitiveness?

I can only offer old words, like salt on a shelf, meant to season the lives we lead and give them purpose. These are my words: service, remembrance, commitment—both to people and ideals—and finally, Koinonia, the matrix of shared life, the washing of feet, sharing of bread, shedding of tears, stranger-befriended, continually reconciling kind of community.

These are only a few of the words, but I give them to you today. Free.

SPENDING TIME WITH MY BABY

Pat Jobe

Several people in the music business made good money off a song that advised, "If you can't be with the one you love, love the one you're with." It's a dandy little melody, and, of course, that kind of thinking created what we now remember as the sexual revolution. For those of you who may have missed it, it was that great testosterone spill of the 1960s and '70s that gave us millions of broken hearts, homes, and single heads-of-households. It was the wholesale marketing of cynicism, cheap thrills, and corruption.

Still, if you could desexualize the song, the sentiment is sublime. "Love the one you're with" sounds remarkably like, "Love one another," and that, my beloved radio relatives, is in the Bible.

But the heart of this commentary springs, alas, from that phrase in the song, "If you can't be with the one you love . . ." And I cannot. After 15 months of marriage to Patricia Allen Manning Jobe—a woman who loves me just the way I am, who has no criticism of my dancing, my libido, my politics, my religion, or my propensity to make loud noises in public places— I find one more detail is to be worked out. I don't get to see enough of her. We both work long hours, she in South Carolina, me in North Carolina. I work two jobs. She gets paid to do the work of one and does two. It's a sad indictment of a reckless youth spent pursuing the lessons of life instead of enough money to be with the ones we love.

So I have a vow for you, beloved listeners, you who loom just beyond the speakers of your radios. I'm going to get rich so I can spend more time with my baby and our children and our extended families and our friends. You see, love is all we really have time for. Life is so short.

MAKING LISTS

Meg Barnhouse

I love making lists. It gives me the illusion of being organized, which is almost as good as actually being organized.

One night in college, my roommate was stomping around muttering about all the things she felt guilty about. We had been writing things on the walls of our room that year because the whole dormitory was being gutted for renovation the following summer.

I said, "Why don't you write a guilt list on the wall?" She grabbed a pen, stalked over to the wall where a large quilt was hanging, lifted it away from the wall to get underneath, and wrote furiously. I decided I felt guilty about a few things, too, and got under the other end of the quilt and wrote my own list.

Things were easier to deal with in blue ink on a white wall, and that winter we wrote lists of all kinds—our fears, our hopes, needs, wants, resentments, things we loved about our lives. The confidential ones were under the hanging quilt, and the regular ones were right out in plain sight. Soon our friends were writing lists on the walls, in our rooms and in theirs. I hope the construction people had fun reading the walls before they hammered them down.

I have a problem with lists, though: I love checking things off. I know you're supposed to write things that need to be done at the beginning of the day and then, at the end of the day, check off what you have accomplished, but there is a rebel inside me who likes to beat the system. I started breaking down each task into smaller ones so I could check off more things. Instead of "Finish taxes," I would write: "Find check registers. Open envelope from IRS. Add numbers in expense book. Cry. Scream. Call accountant."

Finally I was just writing a list at the end of the day of what I had actually done and then checking off every item right then. That worked much better. I was happy. Not really organized, but happy.

When I feel fat or boring, I write lists of my good habits. Once I was having a bad self-image day. I think I had made the mistake of reading my high school alumnae bulletin about all the women in my graduating class starting their own companies, being mayors of large towns, building sailboats in their garages with the help of their brilliant children and sailing to Ecuador to do medical mission work with their loving and wealthy husbands.

Anyway, maybe that was what started the bad self-image day, or maybe I had been reading a magazine article about Danielle Steele, who had just finished her 40th best-seller and birthed her seventh child, remaining thin and beautiful as she cares for her children at home all day and writing at night when everyone goes to sleep and is a gourmet cook, and I thought: "That woman must be on drugs," and then I collapsed into feeling terrible about myself. I had to take myself in hand and make a list of good things about me. It started off with "Not on drugs. Wear my seat belt. Don't smoke." I felt better. Then, just for good measure, I checked everything off with a big check.

I wonder if Danielle Steele makes lists: "Stay thin, finish best-seller, bake cookies for little Lisa's third grade classroom, clean my fabulous house myself without the help of a maid, glam up for book jacket photograph, give magazine interview that will make hundreds of women across the country want to shoot themselves." Check, check, check . . .

Wait, I have to make another list: Stop reading alumnae news, stop reading articles about Danielle Steele and Martha Stewart, stop comparing your insides to their outsides, be a good enough mother, fall madly in love, shape a wild and full life that you want to live with everything that is in you. Check, check, check, check. I feel better already.

BRAIN CLERKS

_____ Kim Taylor

When I think about writing, I don't think about where ideas come from. Occasionally, a friend will ask what made me think of something.

My friend, Betsy Warren, asked her daughter, Kate, one night what made her think of something. Betsy's children are very patient with her and always carefully explain difficult concepts in ways she can understand. Kate said, "You know how you flip though the channels on the TV and stop at something. Well, I was flipping through the channels in my brain . . ."

Kate obviously has more control over her equipment than I do mine. I think of my brain as a filing system owned and operated by a couple of file-clerking masters.

These masters are kind and patient—just like Betsy's kids. And they seem weirdly obsessive. They don't tend to hold onto things they think most everyone would keep. They gravitate toward the obscure.

Sometimes the clerks send me something just because it hasn't come up lately. It's as if they run across it looking for something else and say, "You know, she hasn't seen this in a while. Send it with this."

I don't want to malign them in any way. But there are times when I ask for something that I'm sure is there somewhere and nothing comes. I have an image of them standing around, scratching their heads saying, "Now where did we put that? Did we file that under garages or metaphysics?"

Once in a while when they can't find what I've asked for—or maybe they've misunderstood my request—they'll send something they think is close. Like the time somebody asked me a question about Diane Fosse. They kept sending me information on Diane Feinstein. The only thing these two women have in common is that they share the same first name. As soon as someone else said something about apes, I heard the "oops" from the file room, and they sent the right stuff.

And my clerks can be quite the little rascals. I think when they get bored and run out of coffee, or maybe they've had a little too much coffee, they just start flashing things up. I'm sitting somewhere trying to have a mundane conversation, and these images from Kwondo land start dancing across my brain. Unfortunately, the images are usually more interesting than the conversation, and my eyes glaze over.

When I was considering graduate school, I had to take the Miller's Analogies Test. I was a little concerned because all through grade school, I had noticed that my analogies were never quite the same as anyone else's. When I showed the clerks the analogies, I had to wait a good three minutes for the laughter to subside. Now when I try to recall any of the analogies, they send stuff like this: a gold finch is to a persimmon tree as a bulwark is to a A) futon, B) hyperbole, or C) boulder. They pick boulder, but don't ask me why.

Several months after taking the test, I got my test results. The score was some number that related to nothing I knew or understood. But according to the accompanying chart, I ranked in the top third of creation. I was perfectly satisfied, but the file clerks took it personally. They insisted we should have been given points for creativity. I told them they were welcome to take the test over again, but they'd have to do it without me.

When I started making some noise about going to law school, they told me to go and have a big time, but they would not be coming along. We reached a compromise: I didn't go to law school; they haven't asked for any more tests.

THE GREAT PAPERWORK REBELLION

_____ *Meg Barnhouse*

I hate paperwork. It makes me feel blank and incompetent, and I have arranged my life and my profession in such a way that I hardly have to do any. Paperwork does not like to be ignored, though. It paces in its bleak office and thinks up ways to trip me. Here's what it did.

Last February, I was invited to lead a session on grief for an organization here in Spartanburg. I told the person grief wasn't one of my areas of specialty, and she would be better off calling someone else. "No, we want you to do it," she said. "Please reconsider."

It wasn't going to happen until November. In February I have a hard time believing in November. In fact, since November probably would never come, I agreed to do it.

A month ago, an envelope arrived in the mail. It was a large, manila envelope from the organization that had invited me to do the session on grief. In this manila envelope were 12 pages of paperwork. The first sheet was a biographical form. I was to fill out this form, they said. My ordinary biography or resume would not do as a substitute. There were spaces to be filled out for where I went to high school, where I went to college and what was my major. They wanted to know, in seven lines provided, what I had done in my life that indicated I was competent to lead this session. "Hey, you invited me," I thought, beginning the transformation into my alter ego, the Yankee from Hell.

The next six sheets were about the session I was to give. "Using a separate sheet for each learning objective," the instructions said, "indicate the learning objective, the time you estimate you will spend on each learning objective, and the methods you plan to use for accomplishing each learning objective."

The last five sheets were lists of verbs I might want to use in describing my learning objectives and the methods I would use to accomplish these. One sheet separated the verbs into categories: "receiving verbs" like "ask, name, select, and reply;" "responding verbs" like "answer, assist, perform, recite, and comply;" "valuing verbs" like "justify, describe, and propose." There was a separate sheet for "cognitive verbs" such as "memorize, underline, find, and tally;" and a third sheet for what they called "psychomotor verbs" like "furnish, fix, enlarge, and proceed." I felt like I was in the middle of an education major's nightmare. Was there someone who was being paid to compile lists of verbs for invited speakers?

Why would anyone invite a person to come teach them something if they're afraid you don't know enough verbs? I called the office of the person who had invited me to come talk. That woman was on vacation, so I left a message on her machine. In the message I indicated quite calmly and sweetly that no one had told me when I agreed to do this about the pile of paperwork that was involved. If they wanted me to come speak I would be happy to, but I was not going to fill out a stack of juvenile, useless, make-work forms; it was extremely bad manners to do this to a person.

A nice social worker called me back. She had on the voice they use for dealing with crazy people. It turns out she was someone I used to go to church with. She dropped the crazy-person voice and told me that this particular group's paperwork drove everybody in the office to distraction.

These poor people do so much paperwork it hadn't occurred to anyone that 12 pages might be felt as a burden. She was sweetly reasonable and apologetic, and I knew if I didn't do it she would be the one to suffer, not the person up in the statewide organization who has the manners problem. I filled out the paperwork, but I'm not happy about it. The woman I plan to become would know just what to do. Maybe she could figure out how to make the proper person suffer. Maybe she could laugh. Maybe she could foment a rebellion. That's it! The Great Paperwork Rebellion. I'll start formulating my objectives. What verbs could I suggest? Tear, erase, agitate, refuse, enjoy, free, make trouble, dance, reason, mutiny, dare, defy, resist, oppose. We have better things to do.

PERMISSION TO BE MYSELF
Pat Jobe

I believe I have permission to be myself. My old buddy, Marc LaVecchia, told me once that essays that begin with "I" show that the writer has a huge ego. Yes, that's right. I have a huge ego.

On another occasion, an acquaintance told me that I was conspicuous. I moved, so as to not be conspicuous, but realized later that the essential message of my relationship with this person was, "You are conspicuous." At that point, that had been the message for 12 years. It has taken me another 12 years, but I have succeeded in removing myself from her view almost entirely.

On the rare occasions that I spring into her view, her message remains unchanged. She still pretty much finds me conspicuous.

Finally I have gotten the message. I am outland-ishly, sometimes offensively, often delightfully con-spicuous. You would have found my picture in the dictionary next to the word, except it needs such a large picture. My nose is big. My hair sticks out. My chins are too numerous, and my grin is crooked, hinting at less-than-noble motives. But it is my banter, my chit-chat, the passions that churn like self-righteous charcoal just below the sizzling grill of my talking head that seem to make me really stick out. And finally, I am beginning to accept and love this about myself rather than delude myself that I am not like this.

You see, I've come to realize that I have permission to be myself. It has come to me from the stars. Their message of unchanging beauty and affirmation pours itself into my heart. They say by their eternal attendance at the ball, "You may be conspicuous, or you may have a radical 'personality-ectomy,' but we will not change. We will shine through your best and your worst. We will twinkle, twinkle, and you may find a cure for cancer or commit mass murder, but we will not cease our blessed work."

Thank you, beloved starlight. Thanks a billion, or is it a trillion or a hundred trillion? Thank you for your light, your presence, your beauty, your changelessness, your being the same yesterday, today, and tomorrow. Thank you that I do not feel quite so conspicuous compared to you, but that even when I do, I have your permission.

PERMANENT WAVE

Kim Taylor

Hair? Pat Jobe, did you say hair? Honey, let me tell you about hair.

Imagine being five years old with straight blonde hair, six aunts, two grandmamas, and a world full of Toni Home Perms.

I used to almost envy those little boys whose daddies would drag them to the barber shop for a head shaving, leaving them with their little old ears sticking out like a taxi cab coming down the road with the doors open.

I spent many a Saturday morning, while the boys were outside playing, sitting atop Sears catalogs with my hair being combed, pulled, rolled, chemically assaulted, and styled. I was the only grandchild on one side of the family and the only granddaughter in the country on the other side. All those aunts and grandmamas treated me like a Barbie Doll.

Thirty years ago, all you had to do to be a beautician was to put a sign in your front yard. Back in the '50s, straight razors were the hair-cutting tool of choice. The gum-chomping beautician, her own hair usually in rollers, would pull on a clump of hair and whack it off. She'd get wound up talking to whichever of my aunts or grandmas had driven me there, and first thing you know, there's blood everywhere. I would go relatively peacefully to these backwoods butcher shops until my ears were cut. Then we'd move to the next one. My ears are abnormally small today because they were carved on so frequently when I was younger.

Once, my Grandmother Taylor took me to her beautician's shop. They discussed my five-year-old head of hair like I was headed for the debutante ball. Then, after cutting and styling, they noticed how fuzzy my arms and legs were. They both rubbed the white fine hair growing on my suntanned limbs. They decided something had to be done, or else I might grow up to be just that fuzzy. So out came the straight razor and shaving cream, and they shaved my arms and legs. I looked like a peeled onion.

Fortunately, my mother pitched a fit, and for quite some time, my grandmother was not allowed to take me anywhere. But let me tell you that the trauma of that day lingers still in my heart. I remember the very weird sensation of bald arms and legs.

About 10 years ago, I was coerced into getting a curly perm. The hairdresser wouldn't let me see the hairdo until he was finished. He spun the chair around so I could see in the mirror. I screamed. I'm told they use the story in the local cosmetology school.

My dear friend and hairdresser, Mr. Kit, has great respect for the phobias born of home permanents. I've smacked him silly on occasion for fooling with my hair. Even now, he approaches any new haircut as a diplomat approaches a negotiating table.

Right now, I have what is popularly referred to as a "rat tail." Somehow, I can't bring myself to call it that. Reactions to it are varied. Someone approached me in the grocery store to compliment me. Someone else asked me if I actually had to pay for this haircut.

So, as you see, with all my years of experience and trauma, I still have trouble in the drugstore whenever I have to go down the hair care aisle.

AIR CONDITIONER GUILT

_____ *Meg Barnhouse*

It's getting hot, and I'm feeling conflicted about turning on the air conditioning. I hear people from Old Spartanburg talk with pride about how long they can hold out before turning it on. "Oh," they say in a superior tone, "We always wait until at least the end of June before we use the air." They go on about their 12-foot ceilings and the big oak trees in their yard. They just turn on the attic fan in the cool of the morning and pull in all that delicious air and then shut all the windows and just stay so cool.

If I had the right moral fiber, the properly formed character, I wouldn't need air conditioning, either. My husband, who is from California, has no such qualms. He has been known to turn on the heat in the night and turn the air on the very next day. Whatever feels comfortable. It horrifies me. I tell myself it is because of the money it costs, the usage of energy, the strain on the earth's resources, but it isn't. It's about character.

It betrays something shifty about his upbringing that he doesn't try valiantly to bear up under the heat, to rise above. To endure. Somehow in my childhood I gathered that the highest compliment to one's upbringing was if one could be in the heat and not perspire. I think I recall one of my North Carolina aunts telling me the Queen of England traveled all over the world and never perspired.

I grew up without air conditioning, and scorned it even when we moved to South Carolina. Until the first summer. We were lethargic to the point of stupor, and we were cranky. That summer we went to Sears and charged an air conditioner.

Somehow this is connected to the Scotch-Irish sense of the "fleshly," as opposed to the "spiritual." In my family, "rising above" the need for comfort was a sign not only of good breeding but of a fine spiritual nature.

We live in a blessed land, here in the South. Apart from the occasional hurricane or tornado, the main nuisances we deal with are the heat and the humidity. They ruin our clothes and make us testy. Yet some of us still have an aversion to cooling the air. I heard this on the local news: Now that they've decided that hot weather makes the crime rate rise, they're going to spend $800,000 to beef up patrols in housing projects. Think how many air conditioners that would buy! What a pool that would build! But it wouldn't be good for the residents' characters, I suppose.

"Comfort" was a word that was said with a sneer in my family. Someone who needed to be comfortable was a person of low character. We were adaptable. We admired people who could sit anywhere, sleep anywhere, and rise fresh and flexible. My parents were both preacher's kids, and the preacher's job was often described as "to comfort the afflicted and to afflict the comfortable." It shocked me when a bodywork instructor told me to try to make myself more comfortable by putting a pillow between my knees at night. She told me even the animals make themselves as comfortable as they can.

"Yes, but we are not animals," I heard my Scottish ancestors object in a thick brogue. "We wore woolen kilts and leggings of hide even in the hot summer, and we scratched our flea bites proudly and never needed a bath. We walked to school in the snow and ate oatmeal every morning for breakfast and got spankings for things our brothers and sisters did . . ." Uh-oh. There is a whole chorus of ancestors here. Is there a mistrust of comfort that is carried in the Scotch-Irish gene? A sense that if you have a pleasant day, you'll have to pay for it later? Does comfort make one spiritually weak? Is John Calvin hiding in this closet somewhere?

My brain is now overheated from thinking about all this. I think I'll go sit in front of the air conditioner and cool my good character down.

THE F-WORD

Meg Barnhouse

I want to talk about the "F-word." My children think it's f-a-r-t; I know the one *you're* thinking. The "F-word" makes people squirm and apologize. Some say it loudly, defiantly. Some say it in anger and some in derision. The F-word I want to talk about is "feminist."

What is so scary about this word? Why do so many women preface good, strong statements by saying, "I'm not a feminist, but . . ." I have asked people about this in a totally unscientific and haphazard poll (a T.U.H.P.). They say it's because feminists have been unpleasant in the past. Strident. Unappealing.

That is certainly true. When I was in high school in Philadelphia, I did an internship at a legal services office downtown. Two bra-less women with hairy armpits gave me hell that year, shaming me about wearing perfume and lipstick, about not having the right language or the right opinions. On the other hand, they taught me how to handle the construction workers across the street who yelled unprintable suggestions to us every day. These women said on days when you can't ignore them, when their language is sick or violent, just stick a finger up your nose. "That'll cut back on his fantasies a little bit."

Some feminists in the early '70s made women feel guilty for knowing how to cook, choosing to stay home with their children, wearing make-up, or liking men—even though the stated goals of the movement were to expand women's choices and to affirm and encourage each other's choices. There are disapproving Pharisees and fundamentalists in every movement.

I also remember being shamed in some Christian groups about what I wore or how I acted or spoke. There was as much rigidity there about not toeing the party line, yet the stated principles of Christianity speak of freedom and love above correct belief and behavior. It's funny, though, just because some Christians have been unpleasant, you don't often hear people say: "I'm not a Christian, but . . ."

I am a feminist. For me, that means I try to look at the way things are and ask questions about it. Our world is set up in some crazy ways, and we get so used to it, we don't notice the craziness. For example: Why do you have to know your friend's husband's name to look her up in the phone book? Why do you drive past a family house, and on the mailbox there are little metal letters that say "Steve Jackson," like he lives there by himself? Why is, "You're being so emotional" an insult, and "You're being so logical" isn't? Why are there lots of medications to make people calmer and less emotional, while there are none to help someone who is cold, silent, and distant be *more* emotional? I guess maybe that's what beer and bourbon are for.

Why do people go nuts when you call God "Mother?" Why do little girls who act like boys get approval? Their parents can say, "She's such a tomboy," with affection and pride. On the other hand, what do parents say about their little boys who act like girls? Why can women dress like men and get approval and promotions in the corporate world, but a man who dressed like a woman would get fired?

Is femaleness such a terrible thing? Why do football coaches and Marine sergeants insult their trainees by saying, "Come on, you girls!" Why would a women's coach never be able to shame her players by saying, "Move it, you bunch of boys?" Why does the man at the paint store act insulted when I ask about the "recipe" for sea green?

"It's a formula," he mutters.

These are things I ask myself, and it can be scary.

Once you start pulling on one little thread, noticing little things, asking little questions, the whole thing can start to unravel. If your questions are threatening the way things are, first people try to ignore you, then they ridicule you, then they get hostile. I've seen all that around the F-word. Being a feminist is dangerous to the way things are, but that's the kind of danger I like.

MY DADDY GONNA KILL YOU

Pat Jobe

My office used to be in a battered-women's shelter. To any of you who have had an office in a women's shelter, let me say you walk holy ground. You work in a place the broken come to heal. The endangered learn about safety. The downtrodden learn to remove the oppressor's boot and put on freedom's wings. It's flight school. At times, life itself is flight school.

I loved time with the children. Children always get us, round faces, wide eyes of fear and wonder, tears and laughter, everything made larger by the force of their joys and the depths of their pains. Never say to a person who works in a shelter, "I don't see how you do it." Many of them don't see how the rest of us don't do it. These children played under my desk, drew me pictures. One young man says I taught him to shake hands. I also tried to teach him the guitar. There wasn't time. I pray he still has that guitar.

Another friend was a three-year-old girl. She sometimes rode with me to the post office, the drug store, or to the office of some bureaucracy. The little girl and I rode one day to Smith's Drug Store in Forest City. As I was lifting her out of her car seat, she said, "My daddy gonna kill you."

We always consider that a possibility in the battered-women's movement. Although there has only been one staff fatality in the more than 20 years since the first shelter opened in Houston, the chance that someone might get killed is always out there.

I told her, "No, honey, your daddy not gonna kill me."

"My daddy hurt my mommy," she said as I carried her down the aisle of the store.

"Yes, honey, I know," I told her and looked around hoping no one heard. It's one thing to work in a women's shelter. It's another to confront people with the facts in public.

"My daddy gonna kill my mommy," she said. By this time, I really started to sweat. It was like dating the homecoming queen. I kept expecting her to look at me and say, "What in the Sam Hill are you doing here?" This little girl needed me to say exactly the right things, yet I couldn't help feeling totally inadequate.

"A lot of people love your mommy. We're working very hard to keep her safe, and we love you. We want wonderful things to happen to you in your life." I talked softly, and the little girl listened as we stood in the middle of the crowded drug store.

"My daddy gonna kill you," she repeated. I hugged her.

When we got back to the shelter, a staff member, the girl's mommy, and I spent time with her on the playground. We didn't surround her with fear. We let her talk. The incident later came up in court. It helped Mommy continue a restraining order against Daddy. Life goes on. I tell the story today because I keep running into women I knew in the shelter. We visit, talk about old times. It's all very light and friendly, but I know God doesn't want me to forget them, their cause, their reality, all they have to teach us. The other day, I ran into the mommy of that three-year-old girl. We spoke as we walked past each other. I looked to my left as she climbed into the passenger side of a pickup truck. There in the middle of the seat, sitting next to Daddy, was my little buddy.

My heart froze. Fear gave me a temporary start, but I kept walking. I pray the little girl was wrong, and Daddy doesn't kill anybody. Don't blame Mommy. She's doing the best she can. Don't blame me. I'm doing the best I can. Don't blame yourselves.

But don't ever forget them.

"60 Minutes" did a piece on the dowry murders of 5,000 women yearly in India. The story needs to be told. But FBI statistics show 5,000 battered women die in the United States yearly, and we have one-quarter of India's population. I can't forget them, can't stop supporting shelter programs and good leaders in the movement, can't stop praying and believing a better day comes as we work together to make it so.

ANGER AND DENIAL

_____ *Kim Taylor*

Sometimes, it's hard to remember your objective was to drain the swamp.

That's an old military joke. It has to do with being up to your "little old you-know-what" in alligators. I'm afraid I'm in one of those periods. I need occasional reminders: "WHAT AM I DOING?" (But then maybe many of you have the same questions. What *is* she doing?) Actually, it is at times like these that I realize I'm in training.

Believe it or not, we now have foster children in

our house—three-year-old Ms. McGillicuttie and one-year-old Scooter. The trauma of dealing with one of their relatives has really zonked me. It has slam-dunked me back into the throes of my own childhood pain. But most importantly, I've been able to experience the loss.

I feel like I've stumbled onto a great secret. I never hear any of the "experts" talk about loss in relation to victims. But maybe I just haven't been able to hear it.

When our three-year-old's therapist told us that our child was grieving, lights and bells went off for me.

Suddenly, I realized that I had been stuck in the old anger and denial stage of grieving for 30 years. I could not complete one cycle of grieving before I was faced with more loss.

For me, the losses are not great, tangible, recoverable things. The losses are basic: the loss of trust, of security, of support, and of innocence.

As I remembered these things, I began to realize the connections that victims have—how we can spot each other, how women I've never met will tell me within minutes after meeting me that they, too, were victims.

And then I saw the terrible sadness in the eyes of the three-year-old who has become so important to me. She knows we can hurt her. It's what she expects.

So we try to prepare her for everything. We try to let her know what is going to happen, where we are going to be. The little things make security a reality. "You'll go to the babysitter's. You'll play with the kids there. You'll have lunch. You'll take a nap. And this afternoon, we will come pick you up and take you home."

These children have been with us for over five months. Some days are harder than others; people who have children know that. But what most of you don't know is what it is like to love children who are connected to you by fate. Little people who will come into your lives and completely change them and leave. All before you've caught your breath.

Or maybe that is what parenting is all about, regardless of the time frame. Your heart can be swept up—the good with the bad—and all the joy and the fear can be set free by these tiny maniacs.

It never ceases to amaze me that I can be filled with joy by a squeal or a grin one minute and have an overwhelming desire to body slam one of them the next.

And I never stop believing that I have never done anything more important in my life than open my door and my heart to these children.

ONE MORE KISS

Pat Jobe

This is the kind of story that never makes the news:

He knew it would take about 10 or 15 minutes of his already over-scheduled day. He knew he wouldn't get much of a kiss because she routinely pushes herself to the very last second and then flies out the door, sloshing coffee and shooing dogs as she jumps off the edge of her morning toward work.

Still it would be worth it. The day held a very unappealing schedule—writing a paper and finishing a notebook for a class. He would end up mowing the grass and cutting himself shaving, but at that split-second, as he hovered outside their door, dreaming of that one brush of his lips against her cheek, his day held little hope of anything out of the ordinary.

And in fact, kissing her cheek (lips are off limits after color has been applied), is nothing out of the ordinary. He does it as often as he possibly can—passing through a room she graces with her glory, snuggling in front of the television, at traffic lights. At almost every opportunity, he puckers and leans in like a puppy or a politician mythically bussing his baby while torrents of tenderness rush into his heart.

This morning, he just wants one more kiss.

She exits the house like one leaving a fire. He

knows each move must be timed perfectly. As he strolls toward her frantic figure, she shouts. "Good bye. I love you. Have a good day." He knows she thinks that's it. A kiss is not on her agenda. The door of her minivan hangs open by the time he reaches her. Stacks of books, a purse, the sloshing coffee cup are all finding perches inside the van. As she turns to take her seat, he is standing there, the hunter, the heat-seeking missile of kisses.

"Ooh, you scared me," she says. He doesn't speak but leans in and brushes his lips across her cheek. Three, five, then seven seconds elapse, islands of time on the horizon of an otherwise unkissable day. "Baby, I've got to go," she protests. "I'm late, and they're going to fire me if I keep this up."

He's out of the van, and she throws gravel as she speeds away.

He thinks to himself, "They won't fire you. You are the most wonderful creature ever to push grass against earth with the weight of your foot."

Sometimes she asks, "We've been married two years, and we still like each other?"

"Like?" he thinks. "If this is like, then rain is the ocean, and every rock a mountain range."

Oh, baby, I do still like you and expect I always will.

(Note: As of the publication of this book, it will have been five and a half years since Pat married Pam. He still changes his route and his schedule for one kiss.)

THE GUYS

Kim Taylor

I'm working at a computer lab now as an adult education instructor. It is a very cool program, and I get to spend lots of one-on-one time with my students—all of whom are men. Manly men. America's blue-collar workforce. Guys who spit and sweat. Men whose fingernails have become colors that show just how dirty a job can get.

The guys range in age from early 20s to 60. Most are high-school dropouts. And what I'm learning is that these guys think they are dumb.

They are not.

If it's broke, they can fix it. Even if they don't know what it is, what it does, where it was made or why—they can fix it. Sometimes they have to invent tools to take apart machines that were made in other countries. These guys don't read manuals. Sometimes they couldn't if they wanted to. They just usually don't need to.

But they want to be able to.

The older fellas rolled over and showed me their mushy sides right from the start. They are grandpas. They don't have to prove to me how manly they are. I loved them from the first handshake. They can laugh at themselves. They can be proud of themselves and each other. They can show me how excited they are about learning.

I love old men. It may be because I had a grandfather who was really good at being an old man. And I have a friend who is way over 70, and he is extremely good at being an old man.

Younger, tough men are harder for me. And I can be harder for them. But I've been working on just being present with them. Some of them were able to let go of that manly thing really quickly. I first had to pass a few tests. They had to figure out ways to ask me for help without looking like they were asking for help. So I would grumble over the computer with them. I'd try to find something to make them laugh—either at me or at the computer. Then one day, one of them would just ask me for help. Just ask. Right out. "Would you mind helping me a minute?"

"I'd be proud to," I'd say and jump up. And I *was* proud. Proud that they trusted me enough to ask for my help.

But there was this one guy. I kept asking if he needed anything, how was it going—stuff like that. Mostly, he'd just grunt in my direction.

I thought he must be struggling over the lessons, but I just couldn't quite figure out how to get him to let me help. So I'd sit nearby and doodle and try to think about what I could say or do that might seem helpful without seeming too intrusive. I'd still do the little, "how's it going?" check-ins, but I was feeling like a major teaching failure.

Then one day, during one of my "how's it going?" check-ins, he said, "Not too good." I almost missed it. I was ready for the monosyllabic answer. I tried not to double take. I tried to act casual.

"What's up?" I asked, almost choking.

"Well," he began, and he told me about his math problem. Since then, Mr. Tough Guy has become my bud. He comes by to tell me when he can't make it to class. He tells me jokes. Tells me about the latest movies he's seen and whether I ought to waste my time on them or not.

And he's doing very well in his math, which is teaching me that our public education system is not doing the job we expect it to do. One of my students is a math whiz, and he was in special ed classes all through school. He can't read. But he can run circles around me in math. And he has got the kind of memory that has allowed him to pass in the reading world for most of his life. The longer the word, the more likely he is to know what it is.

I'm learning a lot from these manly men. I'm learning how tough you have to be when you think you are stupid. And how deeply scarred many of them were by a system that didn't fit them and wasn't even willing to try.

And I'm wondering what I do with information like this . . .

BEGGING HELP
FROM MY INNER CHILD

Pat Jobe

How am I ever going to get over my anger at kids? How am I? Oh, how, oh how! Ow, wow, wow, ow, ow.

Can you imagine anything more humiliating to admit? I get angry with children. Oh, yeah, I know you know lots of people who get angry with children, and you can remember how mad grownups used to get when you were a child.

But I don't like it, and I don't want to do it any, any, any more.

I'm looking for a ritual, a candle to light, a rock to throw, a cup to drink from, a loaf to break, a vow to take while holding the hand of someone dear.

I've got it. I'll interview my inner child.

You have got such nerve, after all this time to even admit that you have an inner child, but now you want to interview me on the radio, pulease!

It seems that my 13-year-old inner child has shown up for the interview.

Thirteen, schmirteen. It doesn't matter how old I am. You haven't been in touch in years. Now, you're gonna tell me you've been busy.

Pretty lame excuse, huh?

Oh, let's see. You read John Bradshaw. You listen to a John Bradshaw tape. You know you have to do your *inner-child work to heal from unresolved hurts. You do some of it. It's very powerful; you cry.*

Yes, my children tell me I look very disgusting when I cry.

And then you stop. I seem to remember it's been about three years since we've talked.

Well, this is on the radio. Could you hold the embarrassing revelations down to a dull roar?

Oh, ho, now I'm embarrassing you? I'm so sorry big guy. How can I help you?

Well, I'd really like to live in peace with my children especially, but all children in general. I'd like to be a light, loving presence in their lives.

I'm gonna throw up.

Please don't. I think that would require both of us to throw up.

How disgusting. Look, I know you're up a tree on this thing, but I'm mad at the world. I don't understand why it is that I just can't have everything I want as soon as I want it. I don't understand why I have to do anything I don't want to do, and I don' t understand why I can't do everything I want to do.

I hear you saying you're angry.

So, now, you're my therapist.?

What is my job in your life?

Help me, man. Help me with girls. Help me get some wheels. Help me contain this ball of fire that builds up in me and wants to explode.

I'm glad we had this talk.

Don't you leave me for another three years.

Oh, no, I promise. I'll come back to see you often, my hot young friend. You give me hope for my graying, balding, big-bellied self. You know, I've got children older than you now.

Yeah, but you still need me.

Oh, yes. I need your fire. I need your heat. I need your hunger. You remind me how good it is be alive. You remind me that every moment, every second, every breath, every thought, every word, every step, every touch is precious.

You know, I don't understand you, man. But maybe we can dig each other.

I sure hope so, because we're stuck with each other.

GOING TO AN INNER PARTY
_____ *Meg Barnhouse*

I don't know if any of you have this experience, but I find overheard conversations are more interesting than ones I'm part of. Television sounds more interesting if I don't exactly catch what's being said. An unopened Christmas present is always better than an opened one. The inventions I think up while half-asleep are more fabulous than ones my waking mind comes up with. And what's about to happen is more interesting than what's happening now. The thoughts along the edges of the mainstream are more interesting than the ones in full consciousness.

I don't know what to call it when misreading and mishearing things are a source of inspiration and delight. Right now, I think of it as my Inner Poet. I picture her as a tricky, laughing woman who's cross-eyed from trying to see around corners.

Here's what I'm talking about: I heard someone on the radio say, faintly, "It's coming in at the speed of snow." I still don't know what he really said, but who cares? "It's coming in at the speed of snow" is something you'd hear in a dream. What is the speed of snow exactly? It's a Zen koan. The imagination opens and the linear train of thought derails.

Rereading something I had written the other day, I found a typo. I was talking about a dinner party, and had left off the "d." Going to an "inner party" sounds fun, although I'm not sure how you'd get there, who would be invited, and what would be served. I'm pretty sure you'd get to dance, though, and I think once in a while I've heard the music.

Driving home from the mountains one afternoon, I saw a sign for the "Trinity" fish camp. When I looked again, it said "Tri-city" fish camp, but "Trinity" is a better name. After all, Jesus was a fisherman, and since one member of the trinity spent a lot of time fishing, I think it's an apt name. You can picture the disciples at the Trinity Fish Camp, sitting around a paper-covered table, cracking crabs and talking theology, hush puppy crumbs in their beards.

Another time, there was a sign that I thought said, "Children's Truck Stop," and I got to thinking what a children's truck stop might be like. Would children bring their trucks, gas them up, get the windshields washed? Would they buy tiny boots and eat small burgers and pecan swirls for dessert? I know there would be video games.

Overheard conversations are wonderful. Here's something I overheard in the hospital waiting for a friend to wake up from knee surgery:

"I don't know why he wants to kill hisself, he's got all those millions . . . well, that was a long time ago."

"It wasn't that long ago."

"How long has he got religion?"

"It wasn't 'til about six months ago. That was before. 'Course, he's got beefaloes."

If anybody out there wants to write a short story that makes sense of that conversation, be my guest. I'd love to see it when you're through.

I can tell my children have an inner poet, too, because of the Sylvester Stallone, Wesley Snipes movie they wanted to rent: "Dalmatian Man."

I love the interesting things bumping along the edges of the mainstream of consciousness. These glimpses of an inner wisdom flash like fish in a creek, and if I can grab one by the tail, I feel like I have a treasure. I'll keep fishing for them, and I'll share them with you. But right now I've got to go. I'm off to an inner party at the speed of snow.

BLIZZARD OF '93

_____ *Kim Taylor*

There was a blizzard—the blizzard of '93. I know it was a blizzard because the media said it was a blizzard. It just looked like a lot of snow to me.

When I think of blizzards, I think of the Laura Ingalls Wilder stories. About her dad walking home from somewhere with Christmas candy. Of him falling through a snowdrift and staying in his little snow cave for days. Finally eating the Christmas candy. And when the storm cleared—finding he was only a few hundred feet from their home.

We were never in danger of losing our lives—not at least from the storm.

We were without electricity for five days with two small children. We had plenty of food. We had a well to draw water from. We had a wood heater and enough wood. We had a gas cook stove and enough gas. And two small children.

Maybe, if the children had been older, we could have experienced the blizzard as an adventure. But there was no nightlight, and no VCR.

Unfortunately, Day One was evidence of what the next four days would be like (except that our patience was still intact for the first 24 hours). This is what it was like:

The snow and wind are coming from everywhere. The two-year-old, Scooter, is standing at the window, screaming to go outside. We dress the children in everything they own. Scooter takes one step out the door and falls flat on her face. She rolls over and screams that she wants to go inside. We try to convince her to stay out just a little longer. But the snow is already deeper than her legs are long—so with every attempted step, she plunges headfirst into the snow. She is extremely unhappy.

The four-year-old, Ms. McGillicuttie, gets snow inside her gloves. She takes off her gloves. Her hands get cold. She wants her gloves back on. I have to take off my gloves to help her put her gloves back on. She gets snow inside her gloves. She takes off her gloves . . . well, you get the picture.

I lost count of how many changes of clothes, gloves, and socks we went through.

But the blizzard of '93 *was* educational. For example, we learned that a five-gallon bucket of snow will melt down to about a half-pint of water. We learned that snow will melt faster in the refrigerator than it will in a pot sitting next to a heater. We learned that no matter how long the power is out, we will still try to switch on lights, turn on heaters, and run the microwave. We learned that children who are inside want to be outside. And after you spend 20 minutes dressing them to go outside, within two minutes they will want to come back inside—or they will have to pee.

And we learned that five days without electricity is about four-and-a half days too long.

A DRINK OF WATER

Pat Jobe

Every drink of water is as old as the earth itself. And regardless of whether you are a creationist or an evolutionist or someone who really doesn't care, we all can agree that the earth is very, very, very old—older than the pyramids, older than the Redwood trees, older than any treasure, any idea, any spark in the mind of human beings. Indeed, older than human life itself. Water is a daily reminder that our lives are touched by forces far beyond us, forces that stretch far into the past and may well stretch far into the future.

As we revere water, we hold dear in our hearts the very holiness of life itself. As we abuse water, we attack our connection to all of life.

I want you to hear something (sound of pouring water into a mug).

That was the sound of about eight ounces of water flowing from a glass into a ceramic mug. That water has refracted light for a million dawns and dusks. It has crossed millions of miles. It has rained and snowed and sleeted, given life to flowers and corn and pinto beans and the animals that eat that stuff and each other.

It has dripped off the sides of iced tea glasses and sweated down the ribs of lovers on a thousand dance floors. It is older than the hills and fresher than the morning dew. It affords us the chance to bathe and swim and wet our whistles. O, beloved water, that we were as good to thee, as thou hast been to us.

Let justice roll down like waters, and righteousness, like a mighty stream.

EARTH FIRST

Gary Phillips

I was asked to speak at a conference at the Duke University Marine Lab, an interesting tangle of buildings on a little island off the causeway between Beaufort and Morehead City, North Carolina.

The conference was sponsored by the Coastal Land Trust, and I was asked to speak on limited development and timber resources as a way for landowners to preserve the natural character of the land, protect it for their heirs, and take some money from the property. In my own region, I'm considered an environmental developer, and I know they expected me to come to the gathering with spreadsheets and economic success stories, which I did, but I also brought my deep feelings about ecology, my prophetic hat, and my anger.

It was these that took hold as I looked out at the small sea of significant landowners and timber people, many hundreds of thousands of acres represented, embattled wetlands, rivers, estuarine treasures, lowland hardwood forests, maritime woods, and more. Not a person of color in the crowd, not a longhair, not a single kind-eyed academic. These people were looking for the bottom line. I tried to give it to them, in my own way.

I quoted David Brower: "Wilderness made us. We

didn't make it. We cannot make it. We can only spare it and celebrate." And Wendell Berry: "All my dreams rise up from underfoot. What I stand for is what I stand upon."

Then I turned toward the timber industry—that nest of vipers—and began to rail against the industrial model of forestry, particularly clearcutting. "Natural systems are closed loops," I said. "Economic forestry assumes unlimited resources . . . and a convenient sink to throw the thrash in."

I pleaded for a bridge between absolute preservation and high-yield forestry, for protected river corridors, for an economic vision of forestry that stressed maximum-value production over maximum timber-production, long-term gain over short-term greed.

I made the case for sustainable forestry. I gave them 100 reasons not to depend upon clearcutting—economic and aesthetic and spiritual.

I reminded them that our national forest policy began with a philosophy of management aimed at preserving the aesthetic values of the commercial forest even as it was being used as a source of lumber for housing and industry.

After the presentation, several people came up to speak with me, including an older consulting forester from little Washington, North Carolina. "Earth First!" his T-shirt proudly proclaimed, and I commented on it. With a wry smile, he turned around so I could see the message on the back. It said, "After that, we'll log the rest of the planets."

THE WORLD IN PERIL
———————————————————— *Meg Barnhouse*

It is embarrassing how much I like to read the tabloids while I'm standing in the grocery store checkout line. A couple of months ago, I read in *The Weekly News of the World* that our entire planet had been in peril, and I had not even known about it.

Here is what happened: The Chinese government, according to the article I read at the Harris-Teeter, instructed its citizens to destroy the earth by all jumping up and down at the same time, thereby knocking our planet out of orbit. Alert and committed readers of *The Weekly News of the World*, warned in time by that publication, jumped up and down on our side in a timed counter-jump, thereby saving the earth.

It was stirring. When I'm stirred, I get to thinking. I wondered how the alert readers worked out the timing of their jumps—what with all the time-zone differences—but the paper didn't go into details. It didn't mention why the Chinese would want to destroy the earth. Wouldn't all of *their* children, animals, gardens, photographs, shrines, and loved ones be annihilated along with ours?

I am lost in fascination picturing billions of Chinese people interrupting factory and farm work, parking their bicycles, closing up restaurants, kindergartens, and government offices, and listening, poised for the signal to come over the radio: TIME TO JUMP!

I try to imagine the alert readers of *The Weekly News of the World* who believed the story about the Chinese government's plan and the call for a counter jump. I see them calling friends to enlist their help with the jump; I imagine them trying to explain to their friends what was happening. How did the jumpers feel, knowing that there were so many Chinese and so few alert readers of the *News*? Did they wear weights as they jumped up and down in their back yards to make themselves heavier, or did they figure that they were already heavier than the average Chinese citizen? Did they have confidence that their jump would work, or did they call their families together and bid goodbye to each loved one, just in case the earth were knocked off its course and everyone perished in ice or fire?

You know, as I think about this, I have to say that there are pluses and minuses to having a good education. I remember being in Mr. Murray's sixth-grade class at the Roberts Elementary School, hearing him read *The Iliad* and *The Odyssey*. I remember being amazed that people so far away and so long ago had the same feelings, hopes, fears, and desires as the people I knew. I have learned that all over the world and throughout history, people love, eat, and sleep. We worship and dance and sing and fight. Almost all of us want to go on living. If *we* wouldn't jump up and down to knock the earth out of orbit so the Chinese would be destroyed, it is unlikely that they would do that to destroy us. A good education gives me perspective and makes the world seem like a more rational place.

I miss out on a lot, though, having a good education. The world I see is exciting and alarming but, in a way, very different from the exciting, alarming world of the alert and committed readers of *The Weekly News of the World*. I don't get to believe in the 2,000-year-old babies, lamps possessed by the spirit of Elvis that sing "Jailhouse Rock" when the moon is full, and the women who are carrying Bigfoot's lovechild. I don't get to believe in a world in peril that can be saved simply by all our friends jumping up and down in the back yard.

COOL WAR TOYS

Meg Barnhouse

When I was expecting my first son, I promised I would raise him to be free of the first-born child's tendency to be over-responsible and driven, and I would fight to keep him from absorbing any sex-role stereotyping. He was going to be free to play with dolls, free to wear any color that delighted his heart, free to wear his hair any way he chose.

I tried. Really I did. We watched "Sesame Street" and non-violent videos; his dad modeled many wonderful male behaviors. My son was about two when it happened. While we visited a friend and her children, he was going through their toy chest. He stood, bent nearly double over the edge of the chest, and toys were flying as he tossed them out behind him. He tossed out a beautiful doll with black curly hair, plastic boats, pieces of puzzles, a stuffed bunny. Suddenly his body froze; you could almost hear him hold his breath. He straightened up slowly. In his hand was a Star Wars laser gun. He held it high and stared at it, transfixed, as if looking upon the Holy Grail. He kept that gun with him all afternoon; he even rode the tricycle one-handed so he could hold it while he rode. It didn't leave his hand until I pried it loose when we had to go.

After that, he made guns out of cheese, bread,

sticks, and PLAY-DOH. Finally I gave up. He and his little brother now have an arsenal at home that would outfit a mixed band of pirates, cowboys, ninjas, and intergalactic bounty hunters. They love weapons of any kind. Their eyes light up, their faces glow. A new weapon seems to open up realms of possibility, new ways to protect and defend, incinerate and destroy.

I really don't think they're in love with killing and maiming. They're not old enough to grasp that. I think it's the feeling of power, along with the cool noises you get to make up to go with each new weapon.

They make whip noises, sword swishes, laser buzzes; they can make machine-gun noises that I can't duplicate. This bothers me. It's not that I'm competitive with my children or anything, but I've been secretly practicing the machine-gun noise.

It isn't only boys who like weapons. I remember craving cowgirl guns when I was little. I can't remember what my parents said about it, but I don't think I got any. I did have a cowgirl outfit, though, with fringe and silvery decorations. It was almost enough. I swaggered around the neighborhood in that and felt very fetching.

I do think boys and girls are born different, though. My boys like to whack things, throw things, take things apart, make noise, take up space, slam into each other. It helps if I don't think about it as destructive. I have decided to think of it as scientific experimentation. It's as if they are asking themselves, "What would happen if I took this car apart? How far can I bend my brother's plastic sword before it breaks? Will this little lamb with a music box inside still make noise if it's flying through the air? What about when it hits the ground? If I throw it straight up in the air, can I hit that light fixture and make it shake? Look, Mama, the light is shaking! Watch while I do it again!"

In my old days as an unregenerate male-basher, I would have been muttering about testosterone poisoning and the mayhem that is carried on the Y chromosome, but God, laughing, gave me sons.

She knew what she was doing. I don't male-bash that much anymore, except when middle-aged men leave their families for 18-year-old girls. I am developing an appreciation of the male for the species that I didn't have before.

And I have gotten to be a connoisseur of weaponry. There's this one cool sword that makes a lightning bolt noise when you push one button, and the blade lights up and flashes, and if you swing it back and forth, you hear the clanking sound of metal striking metal. I've got to go play now.

NAUGA

Kim Taylor

My friend, Lynn, had her house broken into a while back. Unfortunately, she was at home at the time. Shortly after that, Lynn decided she was buying a gun.

I tried to talk her out of it. I suggested that her gun might have been used against her if she had had one at the time of the break-in. Nope, no good, she said.

Okay, says me, wouldn't you feel worse now if you had shot him?

She thought a minute, Nope, she said.

And that was that.

Lynn took a firearms safety course, got her concealed weapons permit, and purchased a big old handgun. She called me and invited me to go shopping with her. We were shopping for just the right pistol-toting handbag.

The clerk in the department store asked if she could help us. "Yes," Lynn said, "I'm looking for a purse that will hold a .38 pistol. About yea big." Lynn held up her hands to indicate the size of the gun. After clearing her throat and batting her eyelids several times, the startled clerk said just to call her if we needed her. Lynn shrugged and continued her search. Finally, she found one that looked to be about the right size and style for pistol toting. But upon inspection of the price tag, Lynn announced that she had no intention of paying more for the purse than the pistol. With that, we left the store.

Then Lynn developed a new plan. She would buy yet another gun. This would be her portable protection. It would need to be lightweight with just enough bang for the buck. I suggested a derringer. "I want more than two shots," she said.

Then I remembered that once someone had given me a little .25 automatic. It was one of those gifts where you say, "Gee, thanks," and you walk away holding it at arm's length and wondering what in the hell you are going to do with it.

So I gave the little shooter to Lynn. She took it out, looked it over, pulled the clip. "Thanks," says she.

She decides she'll take it to a deputy sheriff friend of ours and have him clean it up and check it out. On her way to the deputy's house, she stops off at our friend Patty's. She takes the gun in and is showing it to Patty. Patty says, "Don't point that thing in my direction!"

"Oh, don't worry," says Lynn. "The clip is out, the safety is on."

Patty says, "I don't care. There could still be a bullet in the chamber."

Lynn says, "Listen, you don't know anything about guns. I've had gun-safety classes. And I'm telling you that you are safe."

Patty says, "Have you checked to see if there is a bullet in the chamber?"

Lynn says, "The safety is on, the clip is out, and there is no bullet in the chamber, and I will prove it to you." Lynn flicks off the safety and promptly shoots a chair.

I get a phone call from Lynn. "I shot my first nauga," she says.

"What?" I ask. And she tells me the whole story. Then I say, "Well, it ought to be easy enough to stuff. But it's going to be a bitch to mount."

And she says, "Well, I'm expecting you to mount it."

So I call Patty. "Patty," I say, "Lynn would like me to come by and pick up that chair she killed."

After much laughing, we were about to say our good-byes. Patty said, "You know, my greatest fear is that Annie Oakley is going to come back and try to wipe out this whole herd of naugas."

Get the wagons in a circle, boys, and keep those naugas in close. Rollin', rollin', rollin'. Keep those naugas rollin'. Rollin', rollin', rollin'. Nauga Hide.

VISIT TO THE
VIETNAM MEMORIAL

————————————— Meg Barnhouse

I didn't care if I saw the Vietnam Vets Memorial. It was January, and my college friend, Julia, and I had already walked the streets of Washington for miles in bone-chilling cold to see the few things that were open. D.C. was a ghost town. The government was shut down because of a budget standoff, and we had already seen the Vermeer exhibition that was the reason for our trip. The Vietnam Memorial was something they couldn't really close, and we hadn't seen it yet. Julia wanted to go, so I went along.

We took the subway to the stop nearest the Memorial, but there was still a distance to walk. The wind was making a mockery of what passed for warm jackets where we came from. I was tired of my teeth chattering. I bought gloves for $5 from a guy with a table on the sidewalk.

We finally got to the monument. A few other people were there, but not many. I had seen pictures of the Memorial; everybody has. I knew it was dug in like a scar in the earth, a wedge of black marble panels with rows of names carved into them of soldiers who died in that war. The pictures did not prepare me for the power of the place. I started walking down the sloping path into the angle of the wedge. There was a slate trench between the walkway and the wall. Brown leaves were lying in the trench. I saw a wreath laid in the trench among the leaves, leaning against one column of names. The inscription on the wreath read: "From the 26th Para Rescue. You are remembered." I would like to be remembered by those who are left when I am gone.

Next there was a program from Columbia High School's 30th reunion of the class of 1966. It was tucked into a plastic cover so rain wouldn't ruin it. Someone had laid the book under the name of one of his classmates, dead at 19 or 20 and unable to join their 48-year-old classmates now grown bald and paunchy. Forever 19 and thin, green, unwise in the ways of the world. I remember starting to cry when I saw the baby picture leaning against the black wall. A smiling infant barely able to sit up yet. Was it a grandchild? I knew it was someone that soldier would have wanted to know.

The names were coming thick and fast now, in rows as high as my head. They had started slowly, like the casualties in the war. This day, three. Next day, five. A year later, 100. Faster and faster the names piled up, names from all of the cultures of the United States: O'Malley, Patel, Sanchez, Santolini. Row on row were piled the orderly stacks of young lives cut off, sacrificed. Maybe those soldiers would have lived to do great things. Maybe they would have done awful things. Most likely they would have led regular lives, paying mortgages, changing jobs, divorcing, going to church, raising kids.

On down a little farther was a Christmas ornament, a tiny evergreen tree with a string of gold beads wrapped around it. A Christmas card was propped next to it, and then a note in a zip-lock bag. I opened the zip-lock and read the note. It said, "Although I never met you, I want to thank you because your spirit is still alive in your son Bob from Grand Rapids. I love him, and he is a good man, and his mother says he got that from you. I wish I could have known you. I love you. Darla." I leaned my head against the wall and sobbed.

At the deepest angle of the wall, at the lowest point in the walk, the names were far overhead, raining down like napalm, searing me with images of youth and death that stuck in my mind and wouldn't let go. Someone had left a cigarette in the trench with the leftover butt of one that had been smoked beside it— as if someone had sat down to have a smoke with a buddy. A bottle of Romanian plum brandy was left there, and a hat from the 32nd Airborne. Babies, brandy, cigarettes, a sense of belonging, the feeling of sorrow. They belong to the living. We reach out our hands and try to offer them to the dead, to touch them, in memory, in kinship.

I have two sons. I thought about each one of the names on the wall. They each had mothers or fathers who lovingly kept the little Thanksgiving turkey paintings from kindergarten made of their child's handprints. They kept the third-grade school pictures, the track award, the perfect attendance ribbon. The loss was too great. I couldn't bear it. I couldn't hold it all in my head. There was nothing to say. I walked back up along the other side of the wall, back into my life. Back to living.

HOW I GOT HERE FROM THE FOURTH GRADE

Pat Jobe

Tom T. Hall sang, "I guess I owe it all to Pamela Brown." Ms. Brown was the witch who ditched him by switching boyfriends. She was also the bewitching twister of fate who sent him away from his hometown and into the arms of more-than-modest success as a country music singer/songwriter.

He guessed he owed it all to Pamela Brown.

I guess I owe some of it to Mrs. Burwell, our fourth-grade writing teacher. Being from the small-town South, we called her Miz Burl, but regardless of what we called her, she rained inspiration on our lives. She was tall and angular with a head of wild, black hair that was cut short and a long, dark coat that hangs in my memory as an article of clothing setting her apart from the other teachers. The rest of the faculty dressed conservatively and looked like what my mother called "well put together." Miz Burl did not look "well put together." Even if Miz Burl didn't smoke, she had that mad, smoker's death-wish intensity that showed itself in her hurling erasers at misbehaving boys and yelling at us to sit down and shut up. She scared us pretty badly, but what the heck, so did most of the teachers in those days. It was a fear that bred us. In part, it was a fear that made us what we are.

Some time before Christmas that year, I wrote a paper for her on mythology. When she gave out the graded papers, I had made an A. The grade pleased me enough, but what she did next blew me right out of the frames. She stood up in all her mad, angular, gigantic, overcoat glory and pointed one bony finger across the classroom and said, "Pat Jobe is a writer. You just wait and see."

Okay, so maybe I exaggerate. I don't really remember exactly what she said, but that's what it meant to my soul. She praised me. She encouraged me. She opened my 10-year-old heart and poured in the hot, molten lava of dreams. She told my parents to buy me a typewriter, and they did.

So obviously I owe some of it to my parents. I owe a mother lode to my pappy, the redoubtable Allen

Jobe, who pushed *The Charlotte Observer* across the breakfast table and said, "Look at what Kays Gary wrote today," or "Look at what Jim Bishop wrote today." Jim Bishop wrote about his father, and I know my daddy dreamed that one day I'd write about him. I have, more times than I can count. My daddy dances, tells jokes, reads the Bible, flirts with women, prays, and loves life. The rest of the stuff he does ain't fit to tell.

And to my beloved mother, Ruth Jobe, I owe so much for all the times she told me I was wonderful. Lord have mercy, I believed her.

She is also a nut.

We recently attended a soccer game with Jackie Rowe, who had never been to a soccer game. He left early with a promise to return and pick up us. When the game was over, Mama, Daddy, and I stood for a few minutes waiting on Jackie.

Daddy said, "We could be in real trouble because Jackie has no sense of time."

It was cold. The wind was blowing. Jackie drove up within minutes.

Mama climbed in the car and looked at Jackie with the loveliest deadpan you ever saw and said, "We've been standing there an hour, Jackie."

So I owe a lot to my mama and daddy.

And to Kurt Vonnegut, who said something like, "I can do nothing about the chaos in the world around me, but I can reduce to perfect order this single sheet of paper."

And to John Gardner, who quoted Wilt Chamberlain saying, "I'd play basketball if it were illegal." Gardner wrote, "Novelists are worse than that."

Yes, I am not only an essayist but also an unpublished novelist. I am unpublished for a very good reason. None of my five novels are very good. Stacked up on the kitchen table they'd top 14 or 15 inches. There are around 1,000 pages of not very good writing.

I'm currently working on four more that I'm certain are very, very much better, although maybe still not good enough.

Another person who has greatly influenced my writing is my beloved publisher at *The Amazin' Shopper*, Tommy Hicks. Hicks likes what I write and calls me the best writer in North Carolina, and nobody else calls me that, so I really do like him very much. He is a relentless champion of doing what you durn well please in this world, and he likes me anyway. It's amazing how you get people to do stuff for you if you just genuinely like them. Of course, genuinely liking people doesn't come that easily to a lot of folks. Maybe that will change as time goes by.

The Rev. Mary John Dye is a genius who writes about Elvis Presley and how people ought not to call themselves Christians if they're going to beat up on gays and lesbians. I introduced her to Jane Pope, the op-ed editor at *The Charlotte Observer*, who has published both Mary John's and my work and also believes Christians ought to restrain themselves from beating up anybody. These two women have encouraged me tremendously. Mary John once said to me, "You're the best writer I know." It was a lie, but I loved it. I honestly believe lying's not a sin if it's done in an encouraging way. You can see why I called her a genius.

My employer, Charlie Milford, and his wife, Marsha, have been wonderful encouragement. Before I tell you how wonderful, let me tell you a story about Gary Henderson, a writer for the *Herald-Journal* in Spartanburg. Gary and I were having lunch one day at the Sandwich Factory on Morgan Square, home of delicious, low-cost nutrition and excellent company. I told Gary I work for Charlie Milford.

Gary said, "Charlie Milford? I know Charlie Milford." He paused for a second and then said, "He has the nicest wife."

You can see why I love that story, but Marsha Milford really is a very nice person. Some people take niceness, congeniality, good manners, and kindness to superlative degrees. These people were all trained by Marsha Milford. That might be a slight exaggeration, but only slight. Marsha is the kind of person you would want around if you were dying, drying out, gut-shot, lightning struck, dumbstruck, confused, or just had a few minutes to kill around a good fire. She, like almost everybody else I've already mentioned, is among the unsung heroes of a world that so often sings the wrong songs.

Her husband did not marry above himself. Indulge me a few brief praises for Charlie Milford despite the fact that he is my employer and none of these words can escape the pollution of that relationship. He made sure I had access to a computer, the same computer on which these words were written. He did this under the pretense that I might occasionally write a business letter, which I occasionally do. But he also did it in the full knowledge that I would write under threat of death and that if I didn't have a computer, I would scribble on the backs of placemats in restaurants and on bathroom walls. His reputation for kindness, brilliance, fairness, tolerance, and shrewd business acumen precedes him, but I thought it important to add to the public record the fact that he made sure I had access to a computer.

Indulge me a few more lines, a few more words lined up next to other words on this sheet of paper.

Miz Burl started the blessing ball rolling. She opened me up like a surgeon and painted my innards with belief in what I do. I really do love that memory. But there was another shot that was the best shot: a golden, clear, radiant moment that shines in my soul more glorious than all the rest.

Pam Jobe, my wife, my sweetie, my sugar bear, the mama of my household, the queen of my heart, rode with me up to Asheville the weekend of March 27,

1994. I remember the date and the year because it was our first wedding anniversary. We stayed at a bed and breakfast called Abingdon Green. Our hostess was asking about our lives, and there in that beautiful Victorian setting with my heart full of love and mush, Pam looked at the woman and said, "My husband is a preacher and he sells advertising for a living. But what he really is, is a writer."

It tumbled across the room like a magical, mystical cloud, broke into my brain and rained into my heart.

Sentimental, overacting, self-indulgent, egotistical, grandstanding, and unpublished novelist that he is . . . what he really is, is a writer.

Oh, me. Oh, my. I'm a fool for you, baby. And I'm crazy. Yes, I'm crazy, baby.

THE YES BARN

_____ *Meg Barnhouse*

I'm doing the final rewrite on my second novel. There is joy in this because it has taken me a long time to finish. There is pain in it too because the novel is as good as it's going to get. I can't make it any better.

I was doing a reading at Barnes & Noble along with a group of other regional writers. Cooper Smith, who read right before me, had written a soul-shaking story about a boy craving attention and love from his father. John Lane, a poet, read after me. His images were delicious as a hot English muffin with real butter and plum preserves.

I brought the manuscript of my novel with me to work on while I sat drinking coffee and listening to the other writers. What was I thinking? They were good writers. What was I doing here? I looked down at the typed pages and slid into a spiral of despair. It wasn't even as deep and profound as a spiral of despair. It was a sink full of the dirty dishwater of despair.

This is the ingredient in creativity they don't tell you about. The dirty dishwater of despair. One writer I know must take 20 minutes each time she sits down to write and drain out all the leftover dishwater in her brain. She writes it all down: "I can't do this! Who do I think I am? There are real writers out there. There are millions of books out there . . . who needs one more? Maybe I should go watch 'The Price is Right' and forget about writing."

Creating takes courage. There is such a strong "No" voice in most of us. "No you can't dance . . . you look stupid, you sound stupid, what a worthless effort." It takes courage to listen to that voice and paint anyway, dance anyway, write anyway.

There is a building I see driving south on Highway 221 I call the "Yes Barn." It is a wooden house that sits catty-cornered to the road in front of a field. It looks like someone used a wooden billboard as part of the front wall. You can see the huge letters standing on their sides as you drive by. To me it looks like the word "YES." I love looking at it as I drive by.

There are so many "No" voices in my head. "No you shouldn't say that." "No, you shouldn't think that." "You can't do that well, you messed that up, you aren't kind enough, you aren't strong enough, you aren't caring enough, you certainly aren't thin enough."

I like the YESes. Some mystic once said God was the "Yes" of the cosmos. I need the YES. "YES, be who you are. YES, you are a good enough person. YES, you have something to say. YES, be angry and let it move you. YES, fall in love. YES, throw yourself into your life."

I like seeing the "Yes Barn." I drive by it, and I roll down my window sometimes and shout back to it "YES!!"

What—tell me you don't shout at buildings now and then from *your* car. I know you do.

THE MEMORY GAME

Kim Taylor

Ms. McGillicuttie got something called "The Memory Game" on her fourth birthday. For the first few weeks, she called it the "bamemory game" because you had to bamember where the cards were.

There are something like 32 pairs of cards in this game. You turn them all face down and play a "Concentration"-style game of turning up two at a turn to make matches. After about six games, we decided Ms. M was psychic and we were both suffering from some serious brain disorder.

We sent the game to the sitter's. She said she had to cheat to play.

Another friend, currently in college, kept the kids one night while we went to dinner. By the time we got back, she was considering dropping out of school. As soon as we told her how badly we'd been beaten at "bamemory," she was fine.

Of course, since Ms. M is so good at this game, she wants to play it ALL the time. She likes to bounce up and down on her little knees and point out to you that she has four matches and you have none.

This presented a good opportunity for me to give a little conduct lesson. "It isn't nice," I explained, "to squeal 'I'm winning—I'm winning.' It makes the person you're playing with feel bad."

It was difficult for her to relate to losing, since she was undefeated. But a couple of days ago, I won a game. Ms. M was distraught. She hadn't let me win. She began telling me it wasn't fair. And she wanted another shot at me. We talked about winning and how you couldn't always win, and that when she was winning, I didn't cry or complain about it not being fair.

But in the next game, as she rolled over me like a train, we did NOT talk about that gnawing need to win. That drive to be the best. To prove something. To whip the socks off your opponent. I didn't tell her of my embarrassing need to conquer a four-year-old.

I told my friend, Tee, the evil woman who purchased this dreaded game, that she would have to come and get whipped. Tee says that Ms. M won because she could relate to the Disney characters on the cards, and once I became familiar with them, they would more readily register in my memory. I jumped with delight on that theory—a pitiful gauge of my desperation. "Really," I asked anxiously, "it sounds pretty good. What made you think of that?"

"Hey, if I'm going to be whipped by a four-year-old, I'm going to have a reason that sounds good."

SET A GOOD EXAMPLE

Pat Jobe

"When we do the best we can," wrote Helen Keller, "we never know what miracle is wrought in our life, or in the life of another."

That is an echo of my mother, Ruth Merelyn "Jackpot" Thompson Jobe. My father often calls her that because he says he hit the jackpot when he married her. My brother and I feel the same way about our wives. How did such ordinary, mediocre, flawed, and fallible men find such magnificent partners?

I'm sure all you married men feel that way, but if you don't, your wives are ready for you to start.

Part of my mother's magnificence is her belief that we should live good lives, not just for the sake of goodness, but for the sake of being good examples to others. This is not an original idea with her. She is quite a student of the Bible and of her own mother, May Coble Thompson, who has gone on to live with Jesus.

My mother is of the old school. I once told her that my brother, Bill, is so much like her because he has such high standards. She said, "You mean we give people a hard time." That was not what I meant, but you get the picture. My mother knows how to have a good time, but she believes it should only be on appropriate occasions.

So we have this legacy from the Bible and from our grandmother and from the church in general that a good life, a life of kindness and moral uprightness, a life of generosity and a life of hard work, are not ends unto themselves but examples for others. This is good. Paul said as much in Romans when he talked about our need not to be stumbling blocks to others. Modern-day Christians use that passage most often to argue against drinking. It's not drinking that's bad, but setting a bad example as a stumbling block in the path of some poor louse who can't hold his liquor quite as well as you can.

This good example stuff is wonderful but only up to a point. I have had a number of people tell me since I've become a Methodist preacher that I'm a hypocrite. They say you've got to quit sinning once you become a preacher because if you don't, you're just preaching one way and living another. But it's impossible not to sin. The Bible is very clear about that. Jesus preached the Sermon on the Mount to— among other things—make this very clear. Sin's a curse upon us ordinary, mediocre, flawed, and fallible souls, and living right is as impossible as threading a needle with a camel's head.

My mother and the Good Lord and Helen Keller would still encourage you and me to do the best we can, but perfection is impossible.

What is possible then? Faith. Not giving up.

Keeping our lives in the road of reaching for the path of kindness and generosity, love and peace, rock and roll, goodness and mercy, low fat and high fiber, courage and decency and clean thinking. Jesus said, "Follow me," and then he stepped out into the boldest adventure imaginable. When we trip, we should get up and follow again. Remember, my mother is watching. And from that great observatory in the sky, my grandmother, Jesus, and Helen Keller are watching, too.

SOLITAIRE

_____ *Kim Taylor*

I'm in a solitaire slump right now. I'm winning fewer games per hour. As a matter of fact, I'm considering quitting my job to work on my average.

Just kidding—sort of. Actually, I'm a little worried about just how much time I can sit in front of my computer, letting it beat me. When I do win, it's like a miracle. Like beating the odds. And when I'm on a winning streak—oh, man.

But I'm sitting here this afternoon in dire need of a nap, the floor needs mopping, dinner needs prepping, and I'm playing solitaire.

I play solitaire while I'm talking on the phone. I got busted not long ago by a friend who asked rather sweetly, "Would you like to call me after you finish that game?" Oops.

Earlier this summer, I was computerless. I went into a solitaire funk. It got so bad, I actually took a deck of cards and cleared space on a table. I sat and shuffled and played solitaire the old fashioned way for more than an hour. As if that wasn't bad enough, I was humming that old Statler Brothers' tune—something about "counting flowers on the wall, that don't bother me at all, playing solitaire 'til dawn with a deck of 51 . . ."

Then I hear this morning on the news that some companies are taking solitaire off all the company computers. And some state and local governments are considering legislation to remove solitaire from all government computers. It seems that our national addiction to this card game has grown with the size of our computers.

I know that I spend more time playing solitaire on my computer than I spend creating anything of use or value. It's second only to my e-mail addiction. It seems I don't have time to sit right down and write myself a letter, but I've got all the time in the world to forward the worst jokes imaginable to people I rarely see or talk to.

I paid $3,000 for this? Let's see, deck of cards—$2. Pad of paper—$1.50. Pencils—cheap. This does not sound like a wise investment.

But I keep telling myself the computer was really for the kids. They'll need it for school projects. They'll need to learn their way around computers and to not be afraid of computers. I've gotten them some spiffy CDs, including an anatomy one that shows what all the parts of the body do. It can show a skeleton walking. I got them Mavis Beacon's typing CD so they wouldn't be two-finger typists. I got them Math Blasters and Word Munchers.

And you know what they do with the computer? They play solitaire.

I work nights in a computer lab. So, as if it isn't bad enough that I spend all those hours at home on a computer, my work involves computers, too. Those computers at work, by the way, have had the solitaire games removed because it seems that the cleaning folks were coming in at night, and instead of cleaning, they were playing solitaire.

At first, the lab tried putting passwords on the computers. But the cleaning folks were smarter than that and managed to find ways to get to solitaire in spite of the barriers. Wow, that has all the earmarks of addiction, doesn't it?

Well, I'd love to stay and chat, but I haven't played solitaire in like two minutes.

THE SECRET OF FIGHTING CHAOS

Meg Barnhouse

I heard a Scandinavian folktale where the god
Odin asks Thor to force the Prince of Chaos to reveal
the secret of fighting chaos. The awful prince, in
Thor's crushing headlock, says, "Stop! I will tell you.
But first, in payment, you must give me one of your
eyes." Thor plucks out one of his eyes and gives it to
the prince, who laughs in triumph and whispers, "The
secret of fighting chaos," his voice rising to a shout,
"is to WATCH WITH BOTH EYES!"

I fight a continuing battle with chaos. Here is a list
of some of the things that are on the seats and floor-
boards of my car this week: six library books, nine
cassette tapes, seven pennies, two pairs of water shoes
my children can wear to walk in streams, a yellow
marker from a fast-food Kid's Meal that looks like a
melting monster, a colored picture of Jesus walking on
the water from Vacation Bible School at their dad's
church, drawings of tanks, monster trucks, and black-
belted ninjas, an insurance ID card that expired four
years ago, names and addresses of women I went to a
conference with last May, a torn packet of
Buttercrunch lettuce seeds, and a gray plastic sword
that squirts fake blood and has been there since
Halloween last year.

"Everything tends toward chaos," says the second law of thermodynamics, the Law of Entropy. The universe is unwinding. Everything falls apart. Things get messy on every level, emotionally, mentally, materially. You get it straightened out, and then it falls apart again. You brush your teeth, and they need brushing again the next day. It's the same thing with making the bed, doing the dishes, exercising, paperwork, cleaning out the car. It's exhausting to think about it.

I have read books on getting organized, but still for me the state of being organized hovers, like a mirage, just out of reach. My problem with those books is that they don't take into account the ebbs and flows of energy and mood. I have days when I'm alight with power, sparks nearly flying from my fingertips, and I have days when the floodwaters of chaos are rising about me, and I am curled up in my chair with a murder mystery, wanting nothing more than to know who done it.

When faced with the chaos my two small sons create, I play the piano. The books say: Prioritize! Make lists! Set aside an hour a day to keep things in order. Break the problem into manageable pieces and do it a little at a time, slow and steady.

I know that works for some people. Me, I like playing the piano. The pages of music are black and white. I know what music is going to come out when I play each page. If it doesn't sound good, I know what to do to make it sound better.

It's not that way with my small children, my church, my therapy practice, or my relationships. I can do the same things on different days, and the results are unpredictable. Something works one day and doesn't work the next. I may know there is a problem, but I often don't have any idea where to start solving it. Getting organized feels like that: amorphous, mysterious, unfathomable.

I trained with a Jungian analyst who said some people's energy flows in a steady stream, and other people's comes in waves. If your energy is fairly steady, you probably can grasp and implement the suggestions in books about organization. If yours comes in waves, like mine does, you have to ride the wave and do the thing you have energy for at the moment. I am liberated by that theory. I spread all my projects out in front of me and see which one I have energy for at the moment. I'm getting lots of things done. I'm still waiting for the wave of energy to clean out my car. It's out there somewhere, and I'm watching for it— with both eyes.

ROCK OF AGES AT THE TAJ MAHAL

— Meg Barnhouse

In July 1985, I was on a bus in the middle of India with 40 Muslims, Hindus, Jews, Christians, Buddhists, and Moonies. We were touring the world for two months studying each other's religions.

We were on our way to the Taj Mahal, four hours from our hotel in New Delhi. The bus was painted turquoise to ward off evil spirits and hung all over with garlands of marigolds. The day was hot; the road was dusty and full of holes. I was sitting next to Gary from Alabama. Gary was raised Southern Baptist but was now a Moonie. We were talking as the bus bumped and jolted us down the road.

I love talking to people who are on the fringes of my religious experience. Hearing about exotic beliefs and strange practices is one of my favorite hobbies. The Moonies certainly seemed out there on the fringe to me, so I had been pestering them to tell me what they believed. We had a good time questioning each other, sometimes debating, often laughing. Gary and I had gotten to be friends. One of the things we all did to pass the time on long bus rides was to look through each other's wallets, perusing pictures of loved ones, mocking driver's license photos, flipping through insurance cards, love notes, and bank receipts.

Another thing we did to pass the time on long bus and plane rides was to tell what we'd be doing this day and this hour if we were home. It was a Saturday, and I was telling Gary that my husband and I would be getting ready to go over to our friends' house for supper. We would grill chicken, eat vegetables with spinach dip, and sit in the dining room under the black velvet painting of Elvis. The painting had been an anniversary gift from us, and they would hang it up on Saturday nights when we came over. After supper we would move to the living room and sing hymns around the piano, starting with the Navy Hymn about "those in peril on the sea," working up to what we called "blood hymns." Blood hymns were the old-timey ones about the blood of Jesus—the ones with the questionable theology and stirring tunes that so many of us secretly love.

Gary said, "I know about blood hymns—I grew up Southern Baptist!" We started singing. We harmonized on "There's Power in the Blood," and "There is a Fountain Filled with Blood," and "Are You Washed in the Blood?" We had a fine time, and we got applause from the Sikhs who were sitting behind us with their long beards, white turbans, and curved daggers on their belts. They sang us some Sikh songs, and we applauded. Then the Buddhist monks from Nepal sitting across the aisle were moved to chant, and the sound of their voices resonated through the turquoise bus, making our breastbones vibrate. For hours that hot afternoon, we heard Russian Orthodox hymns, songs from Finland, Rasta gospel from Jamaica, and a spell for making yourself impervious to fire from a witch doctor named Andre who lives in Surinam with his 10 beautiful wives and 47 children.

These days, when I hear about the peaceable kingdom where the lion will lie down with the lamb, when I read about the clamor of nations struggling toward peace, I think about that day we sang our spirituals for each other, the day when Christ and Shiva clapped for each other and sang harmonies on a dusty road in a turquoise bus hung with marigolds.

WHY I LOVE THIS RADIO STATION

Pat Jobe

Let me ask you a question. Why do you love this radio station? I mean, if you don't love this radio station, maybe this commentary isn't for you. But if you do—and I know many of you do, because I've sat on the pledge table and listened to you talk about how you love it, and I've read your comment cards, so I know, know, know some of you love this radio station—I wonder why.

Could it be you love it for its diversity? You know, that's the secret of this spot on your FM dial. This radio station is literally a crossroads of ideas, musical styles, lyrical interpretations of what is happening in a world that is threatened with the deadly anesthesia of homogenization. One of my college English professors would tell you that I just mixed two metaphors there with the anesthesia of homogenization, but he was boring beyond my capacity to describe without putting us both to sleep.

Yessir and yes ma'am, of course, this here radio station is a virtual river of diversity. You can hear almost anything imaginable if you listen long enough.

In March 1997, I received a letter from some of the people who manage this river of diversity recommending that maybe I should try to get myself a little commentary spot on another radio station, one where my particular brand of diversity might fit their format a little better. They said they would be glad to consider future commentaries from me if I would submit them in writing prior to broadcast. Of course, all of my commentaries have been submitted in writing prior to broadcast for the past eight years, so I didn't really mind their asking for that.

But it took me five months to figure out that those other radio stations really lack WNCW's diversity, and you see, I just love diversity. I love a public radio station that plays two hours of Gospel music every Sunday morning, plays Gospel bluegrass on Saturday afternoons, and then plays the full gamut of irreverent, lampooning, satirical, lyrical madness at every other opportunity. As the character Annie said in *Fields of Dreams*, "All right, America. I love ya."

I do love you, America, and I love this radio station. I have loved it from its inception, from the first crackle I heard on October 13, 1989, from the first broadcast of Radio Free Bubba on October 17, 1989. You see, beloved brothers and sisters, it is *radio* because of that little box we love to listen to. It is *free* because this is America, and in America, and lots of other places in the world, people are free to say what they damn well please. And it is *Bubba* because I believe there is kinship among all us bubbas—male and female, black, brown, yellow, red, and white, old and young, rich and poor, scared and courageous, union and strike-breaker, communist and capitalist, Buddhist and Hindu, slave and free, gay and lesbian, straight and crooked.

I know I am not alone in that belief. I know that appreciation of diversity is at the heart of many of your lives—a deep suspicion of anyone who would say there is only one way. That's why I love you, and that's why I love this radio station.

THE FIRE THAT BURNS IN BLACK CHURCHES

Gary Phillips

I am sitting now on a porch above a rich, Southern wetland, having just worshiped in joy in an African-American Pentecostal church. After a terrifying week of sacred building after building being put to the torch, I think it is time now for me to talk—not about black church burnings—but about what burns within black churches.

I have no right to do this, no authority. I am just a local Methodist preacher who grew up in the red-ground, white trash, poor side of Polk County, North Carolina. But I have been mentored and brought into the fresh presence of the Spirit over and again by African-American congregations, and I have a special and deep friendship with Alston Chapel United Holy Church in Pittsboro, North Carolina, and its extraordinary woman pastor, the Reverend Elder Carrie Bolton. We have prayed together, sung together, preached together, cried together. We call together now with one voice for justice and reconciliation.

The time is too short for me to say all that needs said. I recommend to you Harvey Cox's *Fire From Heaven: The Rise of Pentecostal Spirituality and the Reshaping of Religion in the Twenty-First Century* and

Shirlee Taylor Haizlip's *The Sweeter the Juice: A Family Memoir in Black and White* and *Fire in the Bones: Reflections on African-American Religious History* by Albert J. Raboteau.

What I would like to do is point to and celebrate certain aspects of ongoing traditional African-American worship and church community which I, as an outsider-insider, believe can serve as a basis for transformation in American life. I have shared these observations with African-American pastors and friends, and they are presented here with their support.

The first is what I call radically inclusive spiritual fellowship. At one point, I engaged with Alston Chapel to create a collaborative film about their worship, bringing into their presence many people who had never attended a Pentecostal service and indeed rarely darkened any church door. All—to a single person—called me or stopped me to say what a powerful and positive experience the project had been for them, and several have come back to worship. One young woman was so moved by a meeting at the church that she timidly asked one of the elders if she could visit again. "Honey," Mother Reeves replied, "our church's doors are hung on welcome hinges. Come anytime."

I am not just talking about the extraordinary hospitality within these churches, but the power and influence of women in their congregations, even those remaining that do not yet allow women to preach. I am also talking about the helping hand of reconciliation to those in recovery, in deep pain or confusion, in trouble with society or their families. At Alston Chapel, there is a pew reserved for kids from Three Springs, an alternative camp for juvenile offenders. When that ragged rainbow collection troops into the church, Elder Bolton smiles and says, "Indeed, Christ is with us."

Another "fruit of the Spirit" I want to lift up from my experience in African-American churches is the recognition and affirmation of the full range of emotion and movement in worship. Harvey Cox writes of his experience of worship in a small Pentecostal church in his hometown: "I learned that the imagery, mood, and tempo of a religious service are not just add-ons. They are not superfluous. Human beings are physical as well as mental creatures, and therefore these more tactile elements are part of the substance of worship. And since life itself is so full of conflict and craving, of wild hopes and dashed expectations, any religion that does not resonate with the full range of these feelings and provide ways of wrestling with them is not worth much." At a time when too many mainline denominational churches have opted for structure over expression, the pulsating and healing energy of traditional African-American spirituality is a tonic for people of all ages and of all faiths, as it speaks directly to the heart with the authority of the Spirit.

Finally I want to hold up that aspect of African-American worship that seeks to empower each individual person, regardless of his public standing, education, or wealth. Writing in *The New York Times*, Shirlee Taylor Haizlip says, "I would grow to understand that there, in that place, every single church member was *somebody*. In God's house, in nowhere else, they were CEOs and presidents, directors and chairmen, counselors. In God's house, in nowhere else, they were women of infinite grace and men of profound dignity."

This June, the entire North Carolina Conference of the United Methodist Church rose in fervent prayer in support of the congregations whose churches had burned. I suggest now a further step of support—one that may speak to the heart of our Spirit-fearful, Spirit-hungry culture. If all of white America could now choose to bend our stiff knees at the altars of black churches across the country, could attend worship in support and attention and respect, could stand with open hearts to receive the blessing, could linger after service to bless and be blessed, then a spiritual renewal might sweep our land that will make the Second Awakening look like a Presbyterian committee meeting.

Our task is to gather up and knit together the broken human family. When white people ask me, "What can we do to support black churches?" I say,

"Walk through their doors. Kneel down and pray."

FIREWORKS AT THE WEDDING

— Meg Barnhouse

I dreamed one night that fireworks had exploded and blown a big hole in the church where I grew up. Fireworks and church may not seem to you to go together, but in my family they do.

In the North Carolina branch of my mother's family, we have fireworks at every major celebration: the 4th of July (of course), New Year's, Thanksgiving, Christmas, birthdays, the first and last days of school, and weddings. Especially weddings.

This is in all other ways a dignified and conservative family, filled with doctors, ministers, teachers, lawyers, and missionaries. It was my missionary grandfather, in fact, who brought the custom back from India where fireworks enliven the best festivities. Several of the dignified pillars of the family disapprove of fireworks at weddings, so we have to sneak to set them off. Fireworks aren't the only mischief in the family, but they are the central mischief.

I just got back from a family wedding. On my way

into the church, I heard one of my cousins talking to his two-year-old nephew. "Darlin'," he said, "there is going to be a beautiful lady in that church carrying some flowers. Now son, some of those flowers are for you. So when she walks by you, just run up and grab you a handful . . ."

As the service began, one cousin slipped outside. No one noticed. We practice not noticing; it's part of the protocol. A few minutes later, when my opera-singer cousin was hitting the high notes in "Where Sheep May Safely Graze," we heard the cannon fire. Then, from right outside the open windows came the rapid-fire volleys of the Black Cats that come in strings of 20 or 30 firecrackers. It made an ungodly racket. The entire crowd on the groom's side of the church jumped in their seats and looked around, wild-eyed. The cellist in the string quartet fell off her chair. On the bride's side, my family gazed calmly straight ahead, squinting a little against the acrid smoke that drifted through the windows into the sanctuary. No one giggled. That is against the code. No one even smiled.

At one wedding we had, the minister was told by the mother of the bride about the tradition of fire-works. She did not want any fireworks at this wed-ding. Like we say here in the South, that minister had a fit and fell in it. He instructed the wedding party at the rehearsal on the sacredness of the occasion, a sacredness that was not to be sullied by fun or high spirits. To drive his point home, he told the Old Testament story about two people who touched the Ark of the Covenant without permission. They were struck dead for sullying a sacred thing. The wedding party stared at their shoes. This wasn't covered in the protocol.

At that wedding, guards were hired and posted along the outside of the church building. One string of Black Cats did get lit, but we only heard three pops. Those strings are hard to stop once they get started. I'm imagining one of the guards threw himself bodily on it. There was a brief incident at the reception where an uncle set off his cannon, and his sister—the mother of the bride—called the police. They came and investigated. There was a lot of talking into police radios, but in Kings Mountain, North Carolina, the police just don't arrest orthopedic surgeons in the middle of the day, even if they have shot off a fireworks cannon in a residential area.

My dream was telling me a truth. The fireworks do blow a hole in that childhood church of mine. Each explosion lets in a little fresh air. They supply a welcome balance to the self-sacrifice and stern structure that is so much a part of that religious tradition.

I left that church long ago for a freer and more liberal one, but I honor joy and celebration in any religion. I'm glad to have been taught that the sacred and the silly walk well hand in hand.

DANG, MOM'S A CRIMINAL

Meg Barnhouse

I knew I had made another parenting mistake the day my oldest son's Sunday School teacher told me he'd been bragging that his mom was a criminal. You know the odds against preacher's kids and therapist's kids. My sons are under a triple whammy: their father is a minister, and their mother is a minister _and_ a therapist. I know they're going to break bad sometime, so I thought I would try to minimize the damage. I thought it might work if I pretended to be shocked and horrified at little things. Then they could get the satisfaction of making their mother gasp in horror without having to do anything too outrageous. I may absolutely forbid them to get earrings when I really don't mind that much. When they sneak and get their ears pierced anyway, they can feel bad to the bone without having to knock over a convenience store.

Here's how it all started. One difficult evening, I yelled—well, not really yelled—I spoke with authority: "Put down that Megaman and brush your dang teeth!" Then, struck by inspiration, I said, "Boys, I'm sorry I cussed. I was very frustrated, and I didn't mean to say 'dang.'" Now they think "dang" is a bad, bad word, and we can all relieve our feelings once in a while by letting loose with a good "DANG!"

One day my four-year-old asked me what a criminal was. "Someone who breaks the law," I answered. Ten minutes later, the seven-year-old asked nonchalantly, "Mom, isn't running a red light against the law?" He had been in the car with me the one and only time (I swear) that I had ever run a red light on a deserted road out in the country.

"Yes honey," I answered. "Running a red light is against the law." Dang. I was distracted, maneuvering through the Friday afternoon crush in the Blockbuster Video parking lot so they could rent Double Dragon Battletoads to play on the Nintendo that weekend.

I thought little more about it until the day when my older son's Sunday School teacher took me aside and said. "Oh, uh, Meg—Sam has been telling his friends you are a criminal." She looked at me speculatively, as if something about me was more intriguing than she had previously thought.

Fortunately, my conscience was clear. I could afford to be amused. "Just out of curiosity," I asked, "how did he sound when he said it? Was he embarrassed or did he sound proud?"

"He sounded kind of proud," she said. I didn't know whether to be happy my son was proud of me or worried that he felt a criminal parent was something to brag about.

I explained to Sam that it was very important to stop at red lights, but that some laws are more important than others and that you're not really a criminal if you break the less important laws. I found myself telling him about states where it was technically against the law to eat peanuts on Sunday or to spit on the sidewalk. Then I found myself saying it was okay to break a law if that law was unjust, and I told him about people of honor who had hidden Jews in their homes in Nazi Germany. His eyes glazed over. Sometimes I explain too much.

"Honey, just don't tell people Mommy's a criminal, okay? I'm not."

"Okay." It was easy.

"And Babe, if you're going to tell people that Mom cusses, please promise to tell them what word Mommy uses, okay?"

"I won't tell, mom," he mumbled.

"Son, I don't want you to have to keep secrets. You can tell anyone you want anything about our family. I just want you to be sure to tell it all. So will you be sure to say which word Mommy uses?"

"Okay."

Poor thing. Being a kid is confusing. So is being a mom. Dang confusing.

SATURDAY IN THE COVE

_____ *Kim Taylor*

We'd been working in the yard most of the day. The kids were both going through their scream-if-you-see-a-bug period. Ms. M. came and said she had something very important to show me and it might be a snake or a bug. I took her hand as we walked around the house. I was explaining to her that there is, in fact, a huge difference between a snake and a bug. "There," she pointed under the swing set. "Definitely not a bug."

I backed both kids away from the swings and back around the house. "Annette," I called in my cheeriest voice.

I am not a snake expert. We bought a book about snakes hoping to be able to recognize anything we came upon out here in the cove. Trouble is, I have a tough time looking at the pictures, and I don't want to get close enough to any of those things in that book to recognize them. Sorry, my reptile loving friends, but I am of the "only-good-snake-is-a-dead-snake" persuasion.

Good old brave Annette pulled out the snake book, and—lo and behold—our snake was a copperhead. Rarely do things in the world look like things in the book. In this case, however, they could have had the same mommy and daddy.

"I'm afraid you are going to have to kill it," I told Annette.

"What should I kill it with?" she asked me.

"Well, the hoe would be good, but maybe the axe would be better."

"Nope." She allowed as how the axe handle was just too short.

Hoe it would be.

Now as anyone who lives in the world would expect, the snake was not in a place that you could just walk up, bonk it in the head, and walk away. It was under the seesaw-thingy of the swing set.

The kids and I were in the front yard holding hands while Annette was scoping out her killing field.

"I can't get a good whack at it," she called.

"Of course not," I answered.

"Well, I'd really like to stand behind it, but the seesaw is in the way."

"So, I guess this means you need me to come hold it out of the way?"

"Well, yes, that would be good."

Goody. An accomplice. I could see the tally on my karma sheet going up.

In all fairness to the snake, it was just lying there, minding its own business. We had mowed, weed eaten, and raked the yard, and none of us—adults, that is—had seen it. We did, by the way, praise the children for coming to get one of us once they had spotted this thing.

So, I got a lawn chair to stand on so I could push this seesaw-thingy out of the way. I had to stand on the crossbar of the swings (which I had not done in more than a few years). The kids stood in my chair holding hands while Annette struck her fatal blow.

In an instant, the hoe was buried in the ground. We watched the tail end of the snake whip back and forth. Annette and I decided to let the hoe stay in the ground 'til we were sure that the snake wasn't just spoofing us.

The children stood, holding their breaths—until the hoe came away from the snake. Once they saw blood, they both let go of a scream that you can probably still hear.

After we got the kids calmed back down, Annette decided she would let them help bury the snake. Way cool.

I would like to note here that fish stories and snake stories have the size-thing in common. Of course, this snake was six feet long and weighed 750 pounds.

But if you dug it up now, it would have shrunk—which is a little-known part of the decomposition process—to about a foot long and about as big around as the average thumb. And once we've forgotten where we buried it, it will have become a python that we whipped Indiana Jones style. Just ask the kids how big that bug was.

SAVING CANS FOR JACK BENNY

By the time this day is over, I will have saved an empty aluminum can for my friend, Jack Benny. No, he's not the late, great star of radio and TV. He is instead a partially-disabled American who is my age—making him neither young nor old—who sells aluminum cans for extra spending money. He works seven days a week, despite his physical challenges, and still needs to save cans for extra cash.

I used to sell the cans myself for the extra money. It took a long time to accumulate five or ten dollars' worth, which I would sell and then convert the cash into gas for my car. About a year and a half ago, my wife and I came to the same conclusion: I was spending too much time thinking about aluminum cans. We decided I needed to spend more of my time thinking about ways to make more money. Of course, these would be environmentally healthy, politically correct, spiritually uplifting ways of making more money, but they would still be ways of making more money.

Some of you think me very strange because I think the thoughts that people think make a tremendous difference in the quality of their lives. Of course, I think your thinking that thought is also a very powerful thought.

This is an ancient idea. Buddhist, Hindu, Jewish, Christian, Taoist, and a whole tossed salad of other faiths have attested to the power of thought for thousands of years across tens of thousands of miles. The old proverb says, "As we think, so we are."

With my sweetheart's blessing, I stopped thinking so much about aluminum cans and began giving my cans to Jack Benny. You hard-hearted, rational, mechanical cynics will say that it is just a coincidence that my income has risen about 20 percent during the year and a half I've saved cans for Jack. You will say there is no relationship between my thoughts and my income. You will say income is tied to the economy or luck or the fact that the corrupt culture in which we live doesn't value you as highly as it should and values Michael Jordan entirely too much. But you will not convince me.

I believe there is a direct relationship, that A runs to B and on to C right on through the alphabet. I believe my thoughts are creating a larger and larger income, which I am now using in responsible, loving, creative, and beautiful ways. I believe a big piece in my puzzle is saving cans for Jack Benny.

THE NEW PLACE

Kim Taylor

After moving from beautiful Montford Cove, I lived with a friend in Marion for about six months. Then, as all little birdies do, I decided I needed my own nest.

At first, I was determined to find another dream house. Something beautiful and peaceful out in the country. For a mere $100,000 or two, this dream could be mine.

Okay, new dream. I'd buy a few acres and put a mobile home on it 'til I could afford to build.

I could find land for sale. Lots of land. In chunks. For chunks of money. And no mobile homes were allowed.

Okay, so maybe something even more temporary was necessary. I called my land-baron friends, and they had just the little place I was looking for—until I looked at it. "Do you have anything else?"

Well, they did have this little trailer out in the woods.

"I'll take it."

"Look at it first," my friend said.

And I did and took it anyway.

It really is a nice little trailer—er, mobile home. Two little bedrooms. One for my part-time children and one for me. And just enough room to turn around in the living room, kitchen, and bath.

Apparently, the rental business is not for everyone. I've been cleaning for three weeks now, and I keep finding little prizes left by the former tenants. The handyman, Doyle, referred to them as HOGS.

"Excuse me?"

"Hogs," he said. "Those folks were hogs. Last two tenants to rent this place have been hogs."

I didn't have much trouble believing Doyle. I've been finding boo-boos, and he's been coming over to fix them.

Saturday, my bed went through the floor. Not all the way through. Not all of my bed. And not while I was using my bed as a trampoline. I was just sitting on my bed. And one corner of it went through the floor.

I called my friend, the landlord. "Sounds like you've got a rotten floor," says he.

"Yep, pretty rotten," says I.

"I'll call Doyle," says he.

Me and Doyle, we're getting pretty tight.

Then after a trip to the laundromat, I went appliance shopping. And after I recovered from sticker-shock, I went to my friendly *used* appliance dealer. We made a deal, and they loaded my formerly owned washer and dryer into my truck—where they stayed for two days until I could round up enough people to get them into the house. Where they sat for two days until I could get the right parts to hook them up.

Where they sit now as I wait for the friendly, used appliance dealer to come wade through the pond that was once my hallway to find out why my formerly-owned appliance peed all over my floor.

I needed to mop the floor, but I was planning on the old-fashioned mop and bucket routine.

I'm trying deep breathing. You know, the Zen mindful approach. The "don't let the little things eat your insides up" approach. I've tried playing solitaire. I called a friend. And now, I'm sitting here.

I could go clean the bathroom. Read a novel. Really mop the floor.

But I can't do much of anything 'cause I'm fixated on this hole in my floor, which is too far away from the water to be a drain, and this water in my floor, which is being soaked up by the dirty towels I was planning on having in the washing machine, not under it.

I know, maybe I'll balance my checkbook.

COUNTRY LIFE

Kim Taylor

I'm one of those people who thought the only difference between living in the city and living in the country was street lights and garbage pickup. Of course, I lived in the city. That is until last year at about this time.

We don't have street lights in the country. We have what the power companies cunningly call "security lights." My personal theory about "security lights" is that they give the burglars better light to work in.

When I lived in town, there was a street light at the front corner of my yard. I parked my car under the street light—where it was broken into and egged. The idea of putting a light in my yard out here in the country and paying for it seems a little beyond reason to me.

We don't have garbage pickup in the country. Out here, you save up your trash and take it to the dumpsters. If you live in town, that won't mean much to you. If you live in the country, the dumpsters have a world of meaning to you.

There are rules about the dumpsters. If you are throwing away something that is just a little bit broken—you don't actually put it in one of the dumpsters. You leave it beside them. Sometimes, you even put a little note on the item, stating what exactly it is that caused you to discard it.

If you take good clothes to the dumpsters, you hang them on the edge of the dumpster. Hangers are preferred.

And if you are just taking plain old every-day kitchen-kind of trash to the dumpsters, you don't go after 9 a.m. That's when everybody shops—at the dumpsters. You'll find folks out there with special dumpster equipment—rakes and rubber gloves and stuff like that. Sometimes they are actually standing inside the dumpster. That's a pretty frightening thought for me personally. I'd be afraid I couldn't get out. I'd be in the bottom of that big old smelly dumpster, yelling "Dial 911!"

When I first moved to the country, I was horrified to find people going through the dumpsters to take things out. Now, I view it as another form of recycling. And the scariest part is, just the other day, I almost went through one myself. There was an old drapery rod sticking out of the top of one of the dumpsters. Now the cord off those old drapery rods is great stuff. It's about 20 to 30 feet of good, strong nylon cord. I stood there between my truck and that dumpster eyeing that rod.

"Nope, nope, I'm not going to do it." And I got in my truck and left.

Later, I told one of my friends what a close call I'd had with the dumpsters, and she started to tell me stories about her husband going through dumpsters and finding appliances and all kinds of things that he could fix and use. I thanked her for her support.

I had already experienced the joys of cleaning out other people's basements and bringing it all home with me. But when it was time to move, I couldn't bring all of that really neat stuff with me. The new owner—fortunately for both of us—was only too happy for me to leave those treasures behind.

My great fear about dumpster shopping is that once I start, I won't be able to stop. Oh, it starts out innocently enough—just a little cord off a discarded drapery rod. Then one day, I find myself buying rubber gloves. Next thing you know, you'll drive up to the dumpsters, and you'll hear a woman's voice yelling, "911, call 911!"

GOVERNMENT WAVE MACHINES

— Meg Barnhouse

I have to rant and rave for a minute. I just got off the phone with a friend in Atlanta. I like almost everything about her except her politics. Her views make me crazy. She's out there in that ideological swampland where the far Right and the far Left meet in a queasy murk of conspiracy theories.

Once she gets going, she can murmur for an hour about the international monetary system and how "they" are plotting to control the world economy. It's this "they" that sends me into sputtering rational overdrive. Who *are* they?

She says *they* are sending low-level vibrations through people's computers that change the energy balance in people's bodies.

"They send things through people's computers?" I ask.

"Well, through their modems. When they're plugged in."

"Why?"

This seems to stump her for a minute, but she rallies. "It has been shown that certain government agencies understand that there are people who are operating at a higher vibrational frequency than others because they have done cellular transformation through bodywork and meditation, and they are not operating in a paradigm of fear anymore."

"That sounds like a good thing," I say.

"Yes, but they would rather people be fear-based and more easily controllable, so they send out these waves that change the level at which people can vibrate. Wherever there is a large gathering of people, they send out these waves over the crowd."

"Let me get this straight," I say. "There is a government agency that is organized enough to send out waves over crowds gathered in Spartanburg and San Diego so that they can interfere with enlightened people to keep them from operating at a higher vibrational frequency so they will stay fearful?" I don't know whether to be scared or glad that some government agency has things together that well.

I have worked in government, and believe me, government appears to be run by people about like you and me who ride into work every day on the train and think about Saturday night while they're supposed to be doing the work of the nation. There is infighting between branches of agencies, and there are power plays at every level so petty as to be surreal.

I once sent a stack of documents to be copied. Because of regulations, they had to be sent to a special copying office. It was two blocks down from the office where I was. The runner took three hours to come pick it up. The next day I waited for the copies. Nothing. The day after that, the runner reappeared. He was carrying the original stack of documents with a note attached. He wasn't allowed to wait while I read the note and responded. I had to call in another request for another runner to take my response back to the copying office. I read the note as the runner left. "We cannot copy documents with paper clips still attached." In the middle of my stack of documents was one paper clip holding three pieces of paper together. It took whoever wrote that note longer to write the note than it would have taken them to take off the paper clip.

That is just one story from government. We have all heard about the $250 toilet seats and the CIA guys selling secrets and driving Rolls Royces to work on $60,000 salaries and no one questioning for years where they got that kind of money. Is this the government that has the technology, the desire, and the organization to send waves over large gatherings to unenlighten some people who have done bodywork? I'm sorry, I can't believe it.

I have never worked with any group of people who could pull off something so intangible, expensive, and bizarre for any period of time. Unless there was some fabulous money in it, I can't see it happening. Of course, in 20 years, when my children and I are living in a world full of fearful zombies controlled by a tyrannical World Order, I'll be sorry I made fun of this.

Meanwhile, the picture of a group of government bureaucrats operating wave machines from a corner at the Lilith Fair makes me smile. I feel my vibratory frequency changing. I'm not afraid.

BLISTER PACKS

Kim Taylor

I believe perforated lines are a government conspiracy. Actually, they are only part of the conspiracy.

As many of you already know, frequently the perforated line—marked "tear here" on most commercial packaging—is in fact the strongest part of the package. Anyone who has wrestled a dog food bag, tried to get into a box of macaroni and cheese, or slammed a frozen dinner onto the floor knows that nothing ever "tears here." Coupons. Checks. Any and all forms with detachable sections. But primarily paper towels and toilet paper.

If you do, by chance, get the tear started at the designated point, it eventually veers off on its own. I think Kimberly Clark ought to just make paper towels with a little ear on one corner.

And now we have the evil blister pack. The name alone is enough to cause a wince—and that's before you ever try to get into one.

And as if that wasn't bad enough, there are variations of the blister pack. I think the first ones must have been too easy to use. The easy ones, which you will rarely see, are made of a sheet of clear plastic with little bubbles at neatly spaced intervals. Pills are placed in the little bubbles, and then a thin sheet of foil is adhered to the back. A gentle push on the pill will pop it through the foil, and you are home free.

So, naturally, this design was a dismal failure.

In case you wondered what happened to the torture experts of the world, now you know: They've gone into package design.

In order to keep the blister pack—but make it more difficult—they added a sheet of something to the back of the foil that only slightly resembles paper. There are two types of these: One has a little corner you are supposed to be able to pull up and away from the pill, and the other has a little notch that you are supposed to be able to tear.

You know those perforated-line guys had to have been in on that little notch. As for the peel-off corner, do you even need to ask?

My approach to the blister-pack problems involves scissors or my Swiss Army knife. I rarely use that knife camping, but I find that when attacking a blister pack, it comes in handy.

And here's the real kicker. You usually need to get into these blister packs when you are not well. The cold and flu ones are the worst. And since we are at our worst when trying to get into them . . . well, it is a cruelty beyond compare.

Now you may ask yourself: How or why could this be a government conspiracy? It's simple really. How can anyone even notice what the government is up to, when all the forms you need to get to them have perforations? And all the pens you need to write with are in blister packs! And even stamps—now that you can peel and stick them—still have to be torn apart, and those little corners just won't pop up.

CALL WAITING HELL

— Meg Barnhouse

I used to wish there was a special circle in hell reserved for people who have Call Waiting. I declared loudly that it really should be called Call Interrupting, or Call Evaluating, Call Jumping, or even Call Dumping.

If I'm the one you're talking to when the beep comes on the line, Call Waiting is a challenge to my self-confidence. Am I more important than the person on the other line? Do I quickly try to say something fascinating before you switch over, like Scheherezade in the Arabian Nights, hoping that if I keep you interested I won't get axed? If you put me on hold, switch over to the other caller, and don't come back to me for a while, how long do I wait before hanging up? I have a strong Southern side, so I feel the need to know what good manners dictate in such a situation.

This is the Call Waiting Relationship Barometer.

At the beginning of the relationship, you are so special that your friend won't even switch lines to find out who is on the other line. You both keep conversing through beep after beep. Then there's the phase when your friend needs to switch over, just in case someone is in trouble, but she comes right back to you muttering about how hard the other person was to get rid of. After a time comes the day when there is another call on the line. She switches over to see who it is and then comes back on your line to tell you she really must take this call. You fleetingly wonder if she muttered to that person how hard *you* were to get rid of.

Now I have to go sit in that circle of hell with all the people who have Call Waiting. Here's what happened. One night, when I was hanging out on the phone with a good friend, there came a banging on our front door. A woman from my husband's church had driven over to tell him—the minister—that one of his members had had a heart attack. She had tried to call for an hour and couldn't get through. I felt awful.

I was raised to believe that hanging out on the phone was trashy behavior indulged in by people of low quality. My father had a list of things not done by People Like Us. My karma in this life seems to consist of doing most of the things on that list, and enjoying them immensely: chewing gum, going barefoot, eating Pop Tarts, and now, talking for hours on the phone. I haven't made chicken salad with Miracle

Whip yet, but I am THIS close.

In order to indulge in this new sleazy and characterless habit of mine, I ordered Call Waiting. My problem is the guilt I feel using it. When I hear the beep that tells me I have another call, I can't figure out the mannerly way to switch over to see who it is on the other line. I know, however, that with practice, some day I will hop back and forth between calls like others do.

I am trying to figure out what this karmic lesson is all about. It could be that I have turned out to be an actual person of low quality and character. I don't think that's true. It could be that there is no such thing as a person of low quality, or it could be that you tell a person's character using other measures: by whether they love justice, act kindly, and see clearly, not by whether they make their chicken salad with real mayonnaise. If you have any ideas, call me. I'll be barefoot, chewing gum, and probably eating Pop Tarts. We'll talk on the phone. Until I get another call.

WHAT DID YOU HAVE IN MIND?

_____ *Pat Jobe*

In the Hollywood classic, *Harvey*, Jimmy Stewart plays Elwood P. Dowd, an engaging madman who means no one harm. His disarming ways include a retort to the trite phrase, "May I help you?" He genuinely asks, "W-What did you have in mind?" He is sincerely amazed that strangers might have any interest in helping him.

Permit me poetic license. "W-What did you have in mind? Do I look as though I need help?" I suppose we all do. Why, I can hardly think of a soul who doesn't need help almost every day. It's an interesting thing about people. People who call themselves independently wealthy are surrounded by people who help them. Middle-class people go to grocery stores and restaurants where people help them get enough to eat to live another day. Poor people help themselves and each other to keep their cars running, share baby-sitting chores, and take care of each other in other ways. Why, I don't know anybody who doesn't need help. So "W-What did you have in mind?"

Actually, I don't like that greeting, especially in the business world. Life is hard enough on the trail of business. Why make it harder with standoffish formality? Why not greet people with, "Hello! Are you well today?" "What's happenin'?" "Howdy Podner, what brings you to these parts?" Or varying combinations thereof. Is a little variety too much to ask?

A little soft-shoe or an occasional song might liven things up a bit. I'm game. Too many people with whom I talk, to whom I listen, or with whom I exchange pleasantries, seem bored by their own selections of places to work, decorations, background music, even the very stuff of their lives—the words they say, their expressions, and ways of standing in line.

I fundamentally believe that only the slightest variations in routine can make life more fun, more entertaining, more holy, more miraculous, less dull and boring and hard.

Next time somebody behind a desk or clerking at a store asks, "May I help you?" give them your best Jimmy Stewart impersonation and ask, "W-What did you have in mind?"

EASTERN NORTH CAROLINA

Kim Taylor

Poor old Thomas Wolfe has been quoted a billion times, "You can't go home again." Make this a billion and one.

I'm not arguing the point. Frankly, I've agreed with it for some time. But recently, it took a new slant. One I like.

I'm from eastern North Carolina. Flat dusty fields. Hot, humid summers. The smell of cured tobacco in huge warehouses. Barbecue.

When I came to the mountains of North Carolina, I wasn't leaving the weather or geography—I was leaving behind childhood pain. But those things seemed inextricably meshed. Smells trigger memory. I didn't want my memory triggered.

Yet there was a pleasant surprise on my last trip east. I went there because a member of my extended family was graduating from college. My chosen family and I gathered together to attend this event.

I went because I felt an obligation. I didn't expect to have a good time. I had a great time.

My three-year-old foster child saw the ocean for the first time. She and I squealed and jumped waves, kicked sand, and spat salt water. Her other foster mother, Annette, took pictures of the foster grandparents doting. We ate fresh seafood while we watched the sun go down over the sound in Nags Head.

But that wasn't the real surprise.

The real surprise was how my eyes and heart soaked up the landscape. How familiar! But without the painful connections! My ears hung on the accent I tried so hard to lose.

Meg Christian wrote a great song called "My Southern Home." It goes, "No longer to blame for the pain that I could have known anywhere." Suddenly, without warning, I could appreciate the place, the people.

I remember being so awed by the cultural differences between the mountains and the Piedmont. But after 16 years of inhaling the mountain air, I had forgotten the differences.

And now I am enchanted by them. I want to go back. I want my memories back. I want the ones I indiscriminately threw away with the bad—the baby with the bath water. I want to eat in those places that tourists won't stop. I want to smell the cured tobacco. I want the ocean to tickle my toes and fresh seafood to tickle my tongue.

I felt at home. I felt I could move back there. Even though it gets hot. Even though Jesse Helms is from there. Charles Kuralt, Maya Angelou, and Randy Travis are from there. And I'm from there, too.

In three days, most of it spent in the car, I reclaimed my home. I took back my memories of a place and separated them from the events that had spoiled them.

In trying to get me to forget the past, my father had asked if the good times didn't outweigh the bad. At the time, I was appalled at the question. I gasped out, "No!"

And now, I can happily say, one has nothing to do with the other.

A GOODBYE AT BIG CREEK
Gary Phillips

All this week I have been thinking of my grandfather, Robert Holloway of Yancey County. Some of you might have known him. Among other things, he was the last schoolteacher at Lost Cove, North Carolina, which is now part of the Pisgah National Forest.

I was 13, at a church camp on the Linville River and in love for the first time. I had a dream, asleep in the top bunk by the cabin window. In the dream, my grandfather was showing me through the house, opening every door as if inviting me into some warm mystery. We came finally into the bedroom, to see both the single beds full, and his white head on each pillow. "Why two grandpas?" I thought, but really I knew.

My parents came and picked me up from camp the next morning, three days early—Daddy, solemn and quiet as he packed suitcases in the trunk, my beautiful momma hiding tears. Friends stood around, and I felt something important was happening. I ran to say goodbye to my girl, then crawled into the car, sleeping in the backseat all the way up the mountain.

Suddenly we were crossing the wooden bridge to Aunt Lena's house, and I tumbled out of the car into the arms of Holloways—cousins and aunts and even familiar neighbors touching and holding and talking alongside the comforting sound of Big Creek. I was transported outside of myself, outside of all my selfish 13-year-old feelings and concerns. So this what I'm part of, I thought, and walked inside to eat chicken in Lena's kitchen.

My grandfather's funeral was held in a hard rain, and the old church was too small for all the people who came. Right in front of the church was a flower wreath made in the amazing design of a coon, a stump, and a hound, homage from friends who knew one of the things Rob Holloway loved best.

I remember that when the preaching was over and hymns sung, the family trooped out in the rain to the black cars and rode the short way to the farm—to the last place a car could go before the long walk to the family cemetery. I was a pallbearer, but it took much help to carry the coffin up the last hill in the settled rain. I would remember that moment for many tens of years—men and boys in dark suits laboring under the coffin in the muddy ground, moving a silent crowd up the last hill to the old man's rest, under a spreading pine that looked over Big Creek.

Walking down the big hill after the graveside service, the Holloways gathered as one family for the last time, with the high porch as a center, and Grandpa's swing always full so I hardly had a turn in it.

I could hear the water singing like a chorus and I thought: *Water in the springhouse behind the kitchen. Water in the branch running by the house and joining another coming down the holler by the road to Big Creek and under a bridge, still within sight. Water running and singing with its trout to the Cane River just down the road, and somewhere past knowing to another river, and maybe another and then to the ocean, and the emptying of the world.*

I imagined my grandpa as a part of that mountain water's ride to the sea.

I watched my clan comfort each other on the high porch and under the yard trees. For once, the grapevine swings and the creeks did not lure me.

The preacher stopped by, but nobody welcomed him. The women gave him a plate of food and set him on the steps to talk to some outcast relation. Leavetaking was in stages, and the huge crowd thinned slowly, like the way light changes at the end of a farm workday. Finally, only the family was left, wandering slowly through a house full of food.

I sat on the porch swing when there was room, listening to the soft talk. I thought: *I can see the mountains moving under the sky.*

Later I would walk with my momma back up the long hill to the pine tree over the family cemetery, while the last crow flew over the valley, swimming in the air toward his comfort.

STELLA, THE QUEEN
OF CHICKEN SALAD

Kim Taylor

My grandmother just died.

She was the only grandparent I had left. She had Alzheimer's and hadn't known anyone for years. I had stopped going to see her—too many relatives to crawl through to get to her. And too little of her there once I did.

My grandmother spoiled me. We did things together. We used to say she loved me best of all the grandchildren because she'd loved me longest. I'm the oldest.

We used to sit together at family gatherings and look at her children. I would shake my head and say,

"It must skip a generation." She liked that. It became one of many private jokes we shared.

In some of her last years, I'd spend weekends with her when none of the other family knew I was there. I'd make the five-hour drive, and Stella and I would sit alone together in her apartment and play cards and tell stories.

Usually, she'd have made chicken salad for me for lunch. I'd take her to her favorite fish place for dinner.

When her health began to decline, and she couldn't make the chicken salad for me anymore, she'd buy it and put it in one of her own bowls.

I have that bowl now. It is my favorite.

I didn't go to Stella's funeral in the church back home. That's because Stella didn't go to church. Someone who didn't know her well obviously made the choices about her funeral.

I've seen too many revivals preached at funeral services. I've had to sit on my hands, my teeth grinding as I watched some red-faced fundamentalist bark about Jesus. Funerals should be for telling stories about the person who has died. They should be a time of laughing and crying and remembering the life of the friend or loved one you've just lost.

No one had to tell me that it was a stiff service done by some well-meaning Methodist telling the family to take comfort in the fact that Stella has gone on to heaven.

Several years ago, on the suggestion of a therapist,

I had a "soul" talk with my grandmother. It was explained to me as a way for my soul or spirit to contact hers. Since talking to her face-to-face was fruitless, it seemed worth a try.

I was told to go to a private and safe place. Light a candle. Make a circle of cornmeal around me (for protection) and meditate. I focused on my grandmother, on her name, on her face and finally, I called to her.

It seemed to me that I saw her, heard her, that we talked.

I asked her to forgive me. I had not been a good granddaughter in the last few years. I felt I'd torn the family apart for my own survival. I could not reconcile those feelings. It is why I needed to talk to her. I needed her forgiveness.

Forgive you? she said to me. There is nothing to forgive. I'm the one who should be asking forgiveness.

But why? I asked.

Because I did not protect you.

I don't know how long I cried. I don't know how long I stayed in that place. I can only remember the joy and the tears.

I don't know what kind of mother she was or what kind of friend. But Stella Leigh Climb a Tree was the queen of chicken salad and canasta and the best grandmother in the whole wide world.

MEG'S BIBLE CONTROL BILL

———————————————— Meg Barnhouse

I start to rant and rave when I read about yet another fundamentalist group punishing their children harshly, yelling prayers and Bible verses for hours at people who are tied to chairs, asking members to sign over all their worldly goods to the church, scaring folks to death with stories of hell and demons and the end of the world.

I wonder why they always use those two or three verses from Proverbs that encourage hitting people with the rod. Why don't they ever read the one that tells fathers not to provoke their children to smoldering anger? Call me crazy, but it seems to me that a child who was beaten while verses were shouted at her might develop a hint of anger later in life. Why do they harp so much on the verse about women submitting to their husbands, and they never quote the verse that comes right before it that says, "Submit yourselves one to another?" Well, you see, now I'm doing it, too. I was raised by Bible-quoting people. Because of that, I know the Bible well. Because of that, I don't like to read it much.

I heard a preacher's wife at a youth conference speak to an audience of 200 college women: "Girls," she began in a husky and confidential tone, "you know how much power we have over men." I looked at my students sitting next to me, and they looked at me with raised eyebrows. Apparently none of us had felt particularly powerful in that way. "You know that we can tempt them to sin without even trying. You remember in Genesis when Eve tempted Adam to eat the apple, and he said, 'No, I can't eat that. God told us not to eat of that fruit.'"

And then the preacher's wife, mimicking Eve, said, "Honey, if you want to sleep with me tonight, you'll eat some of this apple." (I swear the woman shimmied her shoulders and bent over to show cleavage when she said "Honey.") I was clutching the edge of my chair with white knuckles, horrified.

If you read the actual story in the actual book, it says only this: "And she turned to Adam and gave it to him and he ate." Where are the womanly wiles? Where is Eve the Temptress? I am furious that so much of what women have had to deal with in this world comes from that stupid misinterpretation of that one story. Later on, Paul the Apostle says that man is superior to woman because he was made first, and she was made second. I'm a logical person, and it seems to me that logically, if you are going to read the story for who is superior to whom, you would see that it was the plants that were made first, and then the stars and planets, then the birds and the fish, then animals and last, Adam. If the ones made first are the ones who should be in charge, then we should all be taking orders from the fichus tree by the front window or from the goldfish in the kids' room.

Some people I know use the Bible like a weapon, shooting verses back and forth at each other, mowing down opinions and assertions in the Battle of Beliefs. Don't even get me started on the folks who use the Book of Revelation to fuel their madness, obsessing for endless years about who Gog and Magog are and who the Anti-Christ is and when the end is going to come.

No one rants and raves from the kindest and most liberal part of themselves. I am no exception. When I get particularly discouraged, I am likely to think along these lines: Because over-rigid and under-educated interpretations of the Bible affect the lives of so many, especially women and children, by encouraging violence and oppression, I propose we have some sort of safeguards concerning who can own and use a Bible.

We have some gun control now, and my Bible Control Bill borrows heavily from that legislation. I'm thinking of a three-day waiting period before you can purchase a Bible so the store can run background checks to make sure you have no prior convictions of child abuse. In that way, we reduce the odds against people thumping on a Bible while they thump on a child. You should have to sign a paper like you do when you get married where you swear that you are not insane, because insanity and the Book of Revelation are a bad combination. Most of all, in order to purchase a Bible, you must have started at least three sentences in the past year with the words "I could be wrong . . ." I'll give all of this some more thought. I would welcome suggestions. And you know, I'm ranting and raving now, so I could be wrong . . .

RECEIVING THE KEY

Pat Jobe

John Denver sang, "Some days are diamonds. Some days are coal." Probably because it lacked poetic grace, he did not write, "Some days suck pond water." But they do.

December 20 had that quality about it. Other than attending a very nice church meeting, I basically wallowed in the mire of snapping at one of my daughters, financial chaos because I manage money poorly, and a desperate desire to make everything come out right in the life of a 12-year-old boy who is our foster son and a very dear creature to my heart.

In the midst of all this emotional pain, in the midst of facing the Christmas deadline, in the midst of spinning so many plates above my head, I sat down in my wife's van and tried to pull the keys out of the ignition.

They wouldn't come. I took a deep breath and prayed. I pray all the time. I pray over everything. Prayer for me is not the self-righteous, self-inflating doo-dah of a religiously prideful hot-air balloon. It is instead the confessing ranting and raving of a wholly dependent baby, searching for the food, searching for peace, searching for the power to live my life in the thundering echo chamber of my own powerlessness. God, help me. Jesus, grab the other end of the line and pull with all you've got. Somebody come change my diaper. Such prayers are almost always answered.

The keys would not come out of the ignition. I thought about the fact that the ignition bears a duplicate key, an abused cousin of some long-lost cousin flung into some black-hole corner where all keys go to hide and frustrate the human race, which depends on them in this bizarre cult of lock-and-key idolatry. The duplicate key, which had always worked before, would not work now. It actually would turn the switch. I could get electricity—just no cooperation.

I prayed again. Thinking was obviously useless. Thank you, God, for everything. This has become a new mantra. Thank you, God, no matter what. Flat tires, cancer, prison, child abuse. You are the Lord God of the universe, and I am grateful for whatever you put on my plate. Amen. Amen. Amen. The key still would not come out of the ignition. Twist, turn, pull, push, no key.

Deep breath. Deep, deep, deep breath. Anybody who listens to public radio knows that deep breathing is an ancient and powerful way of reducing pain and stress. It gets us in touch with our higher powers, leads to deep wisdom, freshens our breath and brightens our teeth. Okay, okay, I'm getting carried away. Deep breath. Deep breath. The key was still stuck in the ignition.

Then, a long-buried memory surfaced: a 1968 Ford Torino in which I had dated in high school, a car that ran and had a radio that worked, a car of cars, a chariot of dreams that sometimes would not release its key unless the automatic gearshift were pulled all the way to the left. I reached up and pulled the gearshift to the left, and it came right through drive, neutral, reverse, and into park.

My sugar bear had left the van in gear. By some miracle, it had not rolled into the neighbor's yard. By some miracle, it had not killed half the cats and dogs and children in our care. By some miracle, God had once again broken into our lives, the promise of Christmas was kept, and I had, in my precious fingers, the key.

Ah, yes, the key.

MAGIC EIGHT BALL

Meg Barnhouse

My children are in the car asking questions of the magic eight ball. "Are these guys cheap boogers?" asks my 10-year-old from the back seat of the car. He shakes the magic eight ball, waiting for the answer to float up from the depths. He is in disagreement with his little brother about the quality of the rock band playing on the radio as we drive to school. I hear him ask again. "Are these guys cheap boogers?" Shake. Silence. Again. "ARE THESE GUYS CHEAP BOOGERS?" Shake. He laughs in triumph. "It says, 'As I see it, yes!' The magic eight ball thinks your music stinks, too!" I'm laughing at how many times he had to shake the eight ball 'til the answer he wanted floated up to the little window.

The magic eight ball has been rolling around on the floorboard of my car for some weeks now. My youngest bought it with money he had saved from five weeks of allowance. It's a shiny, black, plastic ball filled with blue liquid. In the liquid are floating a couple of plastic pyramids with answers on each side, and different answers float up to a round window in the bottom of the ball. You ask a question, then you shake the ball and wait for the answer to appear. You may get "Signs point to yes," or "Concentrate and then ask again," "Don't count on it," or "Cannot predict now."

I'm loving the questions they want to ask it. "Is my brother a dork?" "Is my mother pretty?" "Is the magic eight ball a piece of cheap trash?" They want to believe in it. They want to believe the answers that float up to the window correspond with the questions they ask. I find myself wanting that, too.

I believe in divination. I look for wisdom to come from Tarot cards, runes, and the I Ching. I believe there is something that speaks to us through arrangements of objects in the physical world, whether it is my inner wisdom speaking or my Higher Power speaking, I can't tell. I don't think divination foretells the future; the future is too fluid. I think divination gives you an in-depth look at what is the situation in the present moment. Knowing the situation is good for planning, for changing your behavior, for making informed decisions. It can give you a warning or a caution or serve as encouragement. I have read Tarot cards since I was 15 years old because my Aunt Ruth taught me how. I know lots of educated and cultured people who use the I Ching regularly and derive great benefit from its insights. My Unitarian religious tradition suggests that I approach all things rationally and with an open mind. So I try to approach the magic eight ball with respect. I try.

I keep breaking into a grin. There is somewhat less dignity in a shiny black plastic ball than there is in a beautiful deck of Tarot cards. No scholars have written commentary on the eight ball as they have on the ancient Chinese I Ching. But who says respect has to be solemn? I let myself giggle. I ask it. "Can I approach you with respect?"

I shake the ball and up floats the answer: "Yes, definitely."

I ask: "Are you a cheap piece of junk?"

It answers, "My sources say no."

Now here comes the sticky part. The eight ball has answered with what seems like coherence. I have to decide now whether to ask it a real question, about something I really want to know. I can leave the eight ball alone now and have had a pleasant encounter with the eight ball angels, or with coincidence. Or I can ask it something that matters. How do I decide? If I ask it something important, and it gives a silly answer or an answer I don't want, I have to deal with that. My philosophy and theology say that God is huge and mysterious and not to be confined to a churchly or even a dignified context. My other way of deciding things is to ask myself what kind of old woman I want to become. I want to be the kind of woman who could hear the voice of God in a magic eight ball.

I ask it, "Is a book of mine going to get published?"

"Outlook good," it says. I like this! I believe in taking encouragement where I can find it.

If it hadn't given me an answer I wanted, would I

have shaken it over and over until I got one that suited me better? Maybe. I know that's cheating, but I want to be the kind of old woman who is not above being a cheap booger.

MASS HYPNOSIS

Pat Jobe

One of my favorite editors is my original partner in Radio Free Bubba, Kim Taylor. She has encouraged me mercilessly. If you think mercilessly is a strange adverb for encouraged, you've obviously never been encouraged by Kim. She takes no prisoners.

You have spent part of the past eight years listening to her and know that her mind is literally like a steel trap. But rather than clinching a thought and holding it, her steel trap snaps over and over again, capturing ideas and snippets of information, grinding them and throwing them out like a combination of a blender and a slingshot. Sacred cows are her favorite targets, but sacred dogs and sacred cats would do well to watch their steps. I adore her, and know you do, too. Or if you don't adore her, maybe you should listen more carefully.

And speaking of Radio Free Bubba, I would be nothing without Meg Barnhouse. I'm sure many of you feel the same way. Meg has a black belt in encouragement. She lights candles and places them in the window for us. She wants us all to come home to our very best selves, to the best stories we ever heard, to the finest music, to the best cooking, to the slowest dances, to the richest compassion, to the most articulate cleverness, and to naps and to laughter and to watching it rain through the window on an afternoon when you would have nothing else to do. Meg says she never tires of hearing me sing her praises—so the rest of you will have to indulge me another sentence or two.

I'm going to commit an act of mass hypnosis so that all of you will fall under my spell, and then one of you—the one who knows in your heart that you are the one, the one among you who has known for a long time now that the universe is calling you to some special task—will step forward and hand me a check for $5,000 that I will use to produce a book of the best of Radio Free Bubba. Others of you will begin telling your friends about it and saving up massive amounts of money so that you will buy multiple copies of this book and give them away to strangers you meet on the street.

That's not all. A craze will seize this planet so that all the Bubbas can join together and exult the worth of all persons in places like "The Oprah Winfrey

Show" and the Vatican. Women will become Catholic priests, and statues will be erected to Meg Barnhouse and Kim Taylor and Gary Phillips and Mother Teresa and John Lennon. World hunger will end like an ice cube melting in the grass.

We will create a massive endowment to make sure that no child ever goes hungry, and no disc jockey ever has to beg money for a public radio station.

"Never again," was the haunting promise that survived the Holocaust, but it didn't come true. Genocide survived. Hunger survived. Racism and child abuse and a whole ugly banquet table of human cruelties survived. But there's a day coming, sweet bubbas. There's a day coming . . .

Ya'll stay tuned to this radio station.

THE DAFFODIL RESCUE MISSION

Meg Barnhouse

I saw hundreds of daffodils blooming in front of the house where I used to live. I was dropping off my sons' rollerblades at their dad's. The boys were going to be there with him for the next five days. They go back and forth between mom's house and dad's house since we separated. I left the house with the daffodils when the marriage ended. Seeing them blooming stirred up feelings of loss, guilt, and longing.

When a friend of mine was a girl, she used to pass one house on her way to school whose yard, in late winter, was covered with daffodils. She thought people with so many daffodils were rich beyond imagining. Today she feels rich according to how many daffodils she has blooming in her yard.

I called her one day in March to help me with a daffodil rescue mission. Some land across from the entrance to our neighborhood had been cleared of trees in preparation for a new strip mall. Construction had been delayed, and grass had grown back over the lot where the trees had been piled up and burned. Along one edge of the clearing was a mass of jonquils, narcissus, and daffodils in shades of yellow: butter, lemon, saffron, and gold. Bulldozers don't concern themselves with beauty. I knew, once construction started, the bulbs would be torn up and thrown away.

I decided they had to be rescued. I called the development company to find who to ask for the bulbs. The receptionist didn't quite know who could give me permission to move the flowers. I wound up talking to the company's president. He said go ahead and take them.

My friend and I met at my house on a warm morning. My wheelbarrow made a racket rolling up the street to the place where the daffodils were blooming, the place where the strip mall was going to be. We dug hundreds of bulbs—three wheelbarrow loads. We were wealthy women by the time we packed the last sweetly smelling jonquils onto the pile of plants. Back in my yard we divided the bulbs. I picked a spot and planted them all the next afternoon.

Some of them are doing fine. There is one group, though, that isn't doing well. They never have done well since I transplanted them. I think they liked where they used to be. Maybe they don't understand why they had to move. It's hard to explain a strip mall to a daffodil. I knew if they stayed where they were, they would never have bloomed again.

People say, "Bloom where you're planted," but things happen. Circumstances change. Development is not always controllable. Sometimes you have to move to bloom. It's hard to explain divorce to a child. They are doing okay, moving back and forth between dad's house and mine, but it's a big change for them. Being transplanted brings hard changes—if you're a daffodil or if you're a 40-year-old woman, if you're a wild jonquil or a well-loved little boy.

EPILOGUE: WHY I'M SO CRAZY ABOUT THIS BOOK

Pat Jobe

The Radio Free Bubba commentaries are unpushed. They flow for me. I can't speak for my partners, whom I adore, but when I sit down to write about politics, water, my wife and kids, religion, prayer, racism, cooking with cats, or Elvis, it flows. I love it.

On the afternoon of November 12, 1997, I sat in Linda Osbon's office at WNCW in Spindale, N.C., and absolutely reveled in the file for Radio Free Bubba. Linda describes it as "a file as big as my thigh," and it is indeed a big file. The thing that struck me was how good it all is. I mean, that may sound terribly arrogant, but please recall I didn't write most of what I was reading. The work of Kim Taylor, Meg Barnhouse, and Gary Phillips crossed before my eyes and into my heart. I was thrilled, like a kid in a dream world, and I was transported and delighted.

Books are like hand grenades of the heart and soul. Spread them around, and they can tear down old walls of misunderstanding and distrust. As they explode, things change. I beg you to buy dozens of copies of this book and send them to your dearest friends and your worst enemies. Buy copies and leave them in waiting rooms and bus stations. Will I get rich? Maybe, but even if I don't, I really believe the world deserves this book. It's like loving your sugar baby or listening to really great music. It's good old-fashioned fun.

When George and Libby Samaras got married up in Columbia, Maryland, my daughter, Katie, was the only little girl at the wedding who wasn't a brides-maid, so she hung out with all the little bridesmaids. They ran around tirelessly, as only little kids can do, and when it came time for the bride and groom to ride over to the reception, Katie stood back as the other little girls piled into the limo. Katie watched, grinning with her hands folded behind her and her dress flowing in front of her. George saw her before shutting the door. "Hey, Katie, you want to ride in the limo?"

She scrambled in and rode away, grinning even more than before.

I hope reading this book was like that for you.

Later, at the wedding reception, my son, P.J., who was about 12 at the time, had been begging the disc jockey to play one of Michael Jackson's hot hits. When the disc jockey finally did, P.J. jumped onto the dance floor and cleared it. People from little kids to glorious oldsters stood back and clapped and cheered, and P.J. twisted and turned and jumped and pumped and brought down the house.

He walked off the dance floor, looked at me deadpan, and said, "Okay, Dad, we can go back to the hotel now."

I hope reading this book was like that for you.

ABOUT THE AUTHORS

Meg Barnhouse is in the remedial Bubba program, having been born in Philadelphia to a Carolina mother and Yankee father. She was raised in Wayne, Pennsylvania, and Statesville, North Carolina. She got back south as fast as she could after she grew up, working as a college chaplain, a Unitarian Universalist minister, and now as a therapist.

Meg, who lives in Spartanburg, South Carolina, has two wise, funny, and handsome sons, a good love, a sweet life. Writing is her idea of having fun, as is going out to eat, watching movies, and kicking the big pad in karate class. More of Meg's essays are collected in *The Rock of Ages at the Taj Mahal*, published by Skinner House Press, 1-800-215-9076.

A founder of the original *Bubba Newsletter*, *Pat Jobe* has been published in *The Charlotte Observer*,

Point magazine, *The Christian Advocate*, and many other places. He has won six first-place writing awards from the N.C. Press Association and The School Bell Award from the N.C. Education Association.

Pat became a United Methodist preacher in 1993 after what he calls "27 years of running from the call." Because his pastorate is only part-time, he also works for The Piedmont Group in Spartanburg, where he and his co-workers recycle absorbent mats, thereby keeping waste oil out of Mother Earth.

He has five children, three dogs, and five cats. Two of the dogs and three of the cats he will give to a good home. His wife says it's okay.

Gary Phillips is a writer, preacher, and part-time farmer in Silk Hope, North Carolina. He has been published in *The North Carolina Independent*, *The Sun*, the *Raleigh News & Observer*, *Journeyman* magazine, and *The Missouri Farm Journal*, among other publications.

He fights for the marginalized in the 500-year war against subsistence, and is a Democratic candidate for county commission in Chatham, North Carolina.

Kim Taylor was born in Bubbland: Wilson, North Carolina. In her research as a career Bubba, she has been a teacher, factory worker, industrial sales clerk, social worker, magistrate, carpenter, and pizza delivery person. She, too, was a founder of the *Bubba Newsletter*.

She drives a pickup truck and lives in a small town in the foothills of Western North Carolina. Her two daughters work diligently to further her education and social training. She thinks she's found the good life.

Publication of *The Best of Radio Free Bubba* is made possible by the generous contributions of:

—**Hubba Bubbas**—
Susu and George Dean Johnson

—**Good 'Ol Bubbas**—
Charles Bebko
Shirley Blaes
Connie and Jim Burgin
James Cato
Richard Culler
Mr. and Mrs. Brian Davenport
Patty Dorian
Karen Kanes Floyd
Glenn Fisher and Carol Trivette
Ann Hicks
Tommy Hicks
Dewey Hobbs
Lisa Isenhower
Pat Jobe
Dorothy and Julian Josey
Jack Lawrence
George Loudon
Mr. and Mrs. Charles Milford
Olencki Graphics, inc.
Janice and Murphy Osborne Jr.
Sharon Parker
Karen Randall
Shirley Rawley
Elizabeth and George Samaras
Macon Smith and Martha Jane Reid-Smith
Chuck White
Cynthia Wood

The Hub City Writers Project is a non-profit organization whose mission is to foster a sense of community through the literary arts. We do this by publishing books from and about our community; encouraging, mentoring, and advancing the careers of local writers; and seeking to make Spartanburg a center for the literary arts.

Our metaphor of organization purposely looks backward to the nineteenth century when Spartanburg was known as the "hub city," a place where railroads converged and departed.

As we approach the twenty-first century, Spartanburg is fast becoming a literary hub of South Carolina with an active and nationally celebrated core group of poets, fiction writers, and essayists. We celebrate these writers—and the ones yet born—as one of our community's greatest assets. William R. Ferris, former director of the Center for the Study of Southern Cultures, says of the emerging South, "Our culture is our greatest resource. We can shape an economic base . . . And it won't be an investment that will disappear."

Hub City Anthology • John Lane & Betsy Teter, editors
Hub City Music Makers • Peter Cooper
Hub City Christmas • John Lane & Betsy Teter, editors
New Southern Harmonies • Rosa Shand, Scott Gould, Deno Trakas, George Singleton
Family Trees • Mike Corbin

COLOPHON

The Best of Radio Free Bubba was recorded with another new look for 1998. The 5" x 7" format was magnetically mastered on three fully-operational Power Macintosh® 7100/80s, sporting all the toys of the trade. The Epson® Stylus® Color 3000 printer, a new addition to our production trilogy, brought tears of joy to the Bubbas when the proofs of the book's cover were initially viewed. The first printing of 2000 soft-bound copies are fresh off the presses. The family of AGaramond was used as the text typefaces; Haskel was the display face. Kaufmann brought a personal touch to all the authors' names. Production assistance was made possible through the help of my American friends, Sam Adams, Miller, and Bud; all who made me wiser.